SOLVING PROBLEMS

PROBLEMS

IN CRIMINAL

LAW

Dr ROGER GEARY

First published in Great Britain 1994 by Cavendish Publishing Limited,
The Glass House, Wharton Street, London WC1X 9PX
Telephone: 071-278 8000   Facsimile: 071-278 8080

British Library Cataloguing in Publication Data

Geary, Roger
Solving Problems in Criminal Law
I Title
344.205

ISBN 1-85941-000-6
Printed and bound in Great Britain

Table of Contents

Table of Cases

iii

Table of Statutes

Coping with Problems 1

Students generally perceive problem questions to be much more of a challenge than essay questions. This is because problems almost invariably involve complicated scenarios, sometimes two or more paragraphs long, which require accurate analysis and precise application of the law. Essay questions, on the other hand, often appear deceptively easy, seemingly allowing for the mechanistic regurgitation of material more or less relevant to the issues raised. It must be acknowledged that there is some truth in these perceptions. Essay questions are easier to pass, although it is probably harder to obtain a really good mark, whereas it is quite possible for a knowledgeable student to fail a problem question as a result of an inability to apply that knowledge to the specific facts. Criminal law examiners, a notoriously unsporting bunch, tend to favour problem questions precisely because they demand this sort of rigour.

Often the sheer length and complexity of problem questions are sufficient to induce a state of panic in the hapless student confronting them under examination conditions. Many exam scripts reveal telling indications of such tension. For example, one candidate in seeking to obtain some philosophic purchase on a problem made a Freudian slip by referring to Rawl's concept of the 'missionary position'. Presumably, what was meant here was the 'original position' which is something rather different. This kind of stress is generated by students simply not knowing how to set about tackling problem questions. It can be alleviated by adhering to a set procedure rather like an athlete's warm-up; this routine will have a calming effect and will not allow time for useless panic. The following is an outline guide to that procedure which will be demonstrated in relation to specific problems in later chapters.

(1)   Read the rubric

In order to find out precisely what the examiner wants you must carefully read the rubric (ie the examiner's actual instructions, usually found at the end of the question). This will usually consist of 'Advise A and B of their criminal liability' or the curt 'Discuss'; a command that can be interpreted to mean advise all the parties mentioned in the scenario. Occasionally you may be asked to concentrate on just one aspect of the law, for example, 'Consider what defences might reasonably be available to X'. Look out for a 'sting in the tail' of the rubric which adds a new element to the facts of the 'Would your answer be different if Boris dies ?' type. It is a sad fact that many students forget to deal with the sting in the tail in the heat of the examinations and thus automatically lose the, usually not insignificant, proportion of the marks allocated for that part of the question. To avoid this, highlight the sting in the tail part of the rubric by underlining it or circling it in red; anything to draw it back to your attention after you have dealt with the main body of the question.

(2)   Read the scenario

Read through the whole scenario in order to gain an overview of the problem. Do not worry too much about the law at this stage; simply concentrate on the facts and try to get a feel for the main plot and sub-plots of the scenario. Usually some of the information provided will be incomplete or ambiguous and it is not a bad idea to make a rough note of issues that require clarification at this stage. The following extracts from examination papers illustrate the type of 'open-textured' information that you must keep an eye open for:

Example 1:

> ... L recruited O to his plan and together they went to Z's house. Unexpectedly, Z returned home and discovered L and O. L hit Z over the head with a poker. Advise the parties of their criminal liability.

Here the ambiguity concerns the extent of the injuries suffered by Z, death (any time up to a year and a day following the attack), grievous bodily harm or mere actual bodily harm are all possibilities that require consideration.

Example 2:

> ... inside the shop Andrew looked around to see if there was anything worth stealing. Eventually, he left the store having paid an 'absurdly low' price for an antique vase as a result of a mistake by the shopkeeper.

We do not know whether or not Andrew entered the shop with an intention to steal. This is, of course, vitally important in relation to his possible liability for burglary. In addition, there is no question of his having an obligation to make restitution and, therefore, for s 5(4) of the 1968 Theft Act to come into operation, unless he knows that the shopkeeper has made a mistake concerning the price of the vase and this is also not clear.

The way in which you should cope with this kind of incomplete or ambiguous information is explained below (see legal reasoning).

(3)   Identify the relevant offences and defences

If you are asked in the rubric to advise one person, read through the question again, pausing at the end of each sentence to consider what possible offences that person may be liable for. Note down all these possibilities on a piece of rough paper; they will form the basis of an answer plan. It is important to ignore the liability of other parties at this stage; this will help to simplify the issues and focus your thinking. Once you have worked your way through the scenario in this way repeat the process once again, this time concentrating on any possible defences that the relevant party might reasonably be able to raise. If you have been asked to advise more than one party, repeat the above procedures considering the liability of each party in turn. The student who tries to tackle a problem question by shifting attention from one party to another and back again is rather like a juggler who tries to keep too many balls in the air at the same time.

When you come to consider the various scenarios in the following chapters it would be a good idea to quickly revise and consolidate the relevant areas of substantive law that you have identified by referring to the appropriate sections of the concise revision notes provided in Chapter 8. Once you feel confident about the relevant law you can progress to the next and vitally important stages of the problem solving process.

(4) Define the offences

You can now start to actually write out your answer. Use sub-headings to distinguish the liability of each person you have been asked to advise. Refer to your notes for the list of offences and defences that that person may have committed and discuss each one in turn. This discussion should commence by accurately stating the statutory or common law definition of the offence or defence in question. It is important that these definitions are as precise as the law permits. There are two reasons for this; firstly, marks are likely to be lost for inaccuracy and secondly, you will need to unpack the various elements of these definitions in order to construct an argument as to whether or not, on the basis of the facts provided, they are satisfied. A mistake at this stage will undermine the foundations of the argument you hope to construct.

(5) Engage in legal reasoning

This stage is by far the most important and will have the bulk of the available marks allocated to it. Here is an opportunity to be imaginative, creative and critical. Use the facts of the scenario to argue whether or not the various elements of the offence definitions have been made out. As we have already noted, often the factual information provided in the scenario will be ambiguous or too scanty to justify any single conclusion. Moreover, the offence definitions are not fixed moulds into which the facts can be neatly poured, rather they are themselves essentially fluid, always subject to the uncertainty of judicial interpretation and development. Any discussion of the case law relating to the offence definitions should indicate these uncertainties, provided, of course, that the particular element of the definition under consideration is relevant to the specific fact situation. You should, then, work from both ends, having deconstructed both the law and the facts, reconstruct by arguing for a particular interpretation or extension of the law to be matched to a specific construction of the facts.

3

Many students lose the opportunity to gain maximum marks at this stage because they become victims of their own rhetoric. That is they put forward an argument based on one construction of law and fact and avoid other possibilities. The 'open-texture' of law, together with the ambiguous elements of the fact situation, nearly always provide the opportunity for the development of alternative arguments. The ability to construct and critically evaluate alternative arguments forms the essence of the lawyer's craft. You should present these alternative arguments as strongly as you can and then evaluate them by citing reasons of policy or principle for favouring one conclusion rather than another. It is at this stage that you can inject a critical perspective on the law by, for example, drawing attention to the conflict between a principle favouring individualism and a policy of collectivism (see Chapter 6). Your 'answer' at this stage will nearly always be problematic, that is, arguable; like John Fowles' novel *The French Lieutenant's Woman* there will be more than one ending. Once you have worked through a deconstruction and reconstruction of both law and fact in relation to one party, repeat the process in relation to the remaining parties whose liability has to be considered. It would be foolish to pretend that the above process is easy, on the contrary it requires an appreciation of the subtleties of criminal law and an ability to apply sophisticated intellectual skills of a high standard.

Outline of the book

The following discussions of the various scenarios are designed to 'talk you' through the process of coping with complex problems and, hopefully, assist in the acquisition and development of the required skills. Unlike many traditional 'model answers' their purpose is not merely to illustrate the application of problem-solving procedures, but also to indicate how both the law and the given facts are often 'open-textured', allowing for the development of alternative arguments. In this way it is hoped to correct the unfortunate tendency of many students to fail to appreciate this exciting and creative aspect of studying criminal law.

Although problem questions in criminal law tend to be eclectic in nature, involving many different offences and defences, it is often possible to identify certain topics which are of central importance in particular fact situations. The next chapter demonstrates the application of the above problem solving procedure to scenarios which have as their focal concerns secondary liability and liability for the inchoate offences of incitement, conspiracy and attempt. Chapters 3 and 4 respectively concentrate on offences against the person and offences against property, while Chapter 5 deals with scenarios that are mainly concerned with defences.

In Chapter 6 we revisit some of the earlier scenarios in order to indicate how students can elevate the standard of their work by the judicious use of references to relevant learned articles and by supplementing discussion of 'black-letter' law by the introduction, where appropriate, of issues of principle, policy and political philosophy. It is a sad fact that many students, and, indeed, some lecturers, do not always seem sure about precisely what it is that makes the difference between a good upper-second and a first-class piece of work. This chapter addresses this issue by indicating the kind of extra content that would be required to raise traditional problem-solving from something akin to doing crossword puzzles to the more elevated plane of quality legal scholarship.

A pragmatic list of do's and don'ts is provided in Chapter 7 encompassing such matters as structure, content and style, while Chapter 8 consists of a concise summary of the relevant substantive law in note form. This summary is provided in order that students can gain an immediate overview of the basic rules and principles of criminal law that will, in turn, enable them to better understand the complex and multi-faceted problem scenarios. Often the sheer bulk and complexity of the standard textbook in criminal law militates against this kind of holistic understanding with the result that all too few students emerge from the tangled and thorny thickets of legal scholarship without any clear idea of the territory they have so painfully covered. It is also hoped that students will find this summary of use as an aid for revision purposes.

Inchoate Offences & Modes of Participation   2

The discussions contained in this and the next three chapters are intended to demonstrate how the problem-solving procedure, outlined above, can be applied to a number of different scenarios. It is worth re-emphasising that these discussions are not presented as completed end-products in the form of 'model answers', but rather as examples of the *methodology* to be employed in order to cope with problem situations. Indeed, 'model answers' are of only limited value since they tend to encourage rote learning in the somewhat desperate hope that the student will then be confronted with exactly the same questions in an examination situation. Of course, the chances of this happening are extremely remote; even the most unimaginative examiners tend to never repeat themselves, at least not in precisely the same way. Moreover, having taken the trouble to learn a number of set answers, the ill prepared student is then under great psychological pressure to apply the prepared answer to a factual situation which it does not fit. This disjunction between the problem and its solution is all too obvious and will often result in no, or very few, marks being awarded, notwithstanding that the legal information provided is correct in itself.

However, once mastered the procedure for solving problems in criminal law becomes a transferable intellectual skill which can be applied successfully to the facts of any scenario. You should, therefore, think of this book as your own private tutor who attempts to show you how to build up this over-arching problem-solving ability out of a synthesis of the skills of identification, definition, analysis and evaluation. The following discussions are not intended to provide 'suggested solutions' or 'model answers', but constitute a learning experience whereby the student can develop problem-solving skills by observing their application in a variety of situations.

Many problem questions in criminal law tend to be wide-ranging, covering large sections of the syllabus, nevertheless it is usually possible to identify one or two main areas of concern. In this chapter our attention focuses on those scenarios which raise issues relating to the inchoate offences of incitement, conspiracy and attempt, as well as in relation to secondary liability as an accomplice.

Scenario 1

Roger suggests to Rebecca, his mistress, that they murder Roger's wife Belinda. Rebecca agrees but does nothing to bring the crime about. Roger is supplied with a deadly poison by his old school-friend Boris. The poison was injected into an

7

'after-eight' mint by Roger which he then gave to Belinda. Belinda gave the mint to Jasper, their nine year old son, and Roger did nothing while Jasper ate half of the mint. Jasper then gave the remaining half of the mint to 'Devlin' his pet dog. Jasper and Devlin died within minutes. Belinda is so shocked by these events that she falls into a trance-like state during which she kills the milkman with a rolling-pin.

Discuss the criminal liability of the parties.

Although this question raises many issues even a fairly casual consideration indicates that it focuses mainly on inchoate offences and modes of participation as opposed to offences against property. It is possible to make this kind of broad distinction with most problem scenarios. However, be careful because, as we shall see, even this problem involves some offences against property. Classification should not function as a blinker, preventing us from seeing all the issues, rather it should act as a spot-light, illuminating the areas that require detailed consideration. This chapter will focus mainly on inchoate offences and participation while the later chapters concentrate in turn on offences against the person, property offences and defences. You will require a sound knowledge of the substantive law relating to these areas in order to get the most out of the following discussion of the problem situations. It is a good idea to read over the sections on general principles, inchoate offences and participation in the concise notes contained in Chapter 8 before proceeding with the analysis of the problem.

We will now apply the five procedures outlined in Chapter 1 to the above scenario:

(1)   Read the rubric

'Discuss the criminal liability of the parties'

A familiar instruction from the examiner. On the face of it the criminal liability of all the people involved in the scenario should be considered ie Roger, Rebecca, Belinda, Boris, Jasper and the milkman. However, the more perceptive student will immediately realise that Jasper and the milkman can be eliminated from our deliberations for two reasons. Firstly, they are mere victims and secondly, and more fundamentally, they are both dead. In a sense the last six words of the rubric are superfluous; the above approach would be equally applicable if it had simply read 'Discuss'. Also note the absence in the rubric of any 'sting in the tail' (there is quite enough to do here without any additional complications).

(2)   Read the question

A reading of this somewhat complex fact situation will probably cause several issues immediately to occur to you. For example, Roger's omission to prevent Jasper from eating the poisoned mint and the apparent autonomic state of Belinda when she kills the milkman tend to spring to mind. Nevertheless, it is important to avoid discussion of such matters at this stage. Simply concentrate on trying to get the facts straight; avoid worrying too much about the law at this stage. It is, however, a good idea to identify any incomplete or ambiguous information. As it happens, in this particular scenario the facts seem relatively unambiguous although complex. An attentive student might make a rough note querying whether Devlin really belongs to Jasper or to Roger, whether Roger asked Boris to supply the poison and whether Boris knows of and agrees with Roger's plan to murder Belinda. The significance of these points will be made clear below.

(3)   Identify the relevant offences and defences

Work through the problem sentence by sentence, first identifying what offences each party may reasonably have committed and then again focusing on what defences they may be able to raise. Simplify the issues by considering each party in turn. Do not, at this stage, be drawn into a discussion of liability, merely note the possibilities.

 If the scenario involves accomplices deal with the liability of the principal before considering that of the secondary parties.

Roger's liability

The key word in the first sentence is 'suggests'. This itself suggests a crime, that of soliciting murder contrary to s 4 of the Offences Against the Person Act 1861. Similarly, in the second sentence the word 'agrees' should alert you to the possibility of a statutory conspiracy to murder between Roger and Rebecca contrary to s 1 of the Criminal Law Act 1977. The third sentence is rather more subtle in that it is what is implied that raises the possibility of further criminal liability for Roger. If Roger has requested Boris to supply the poison there is the possibility of a common law incitement and of Boris joining the statutory conspiracy to kill Belinda. Moreover, if Boris has himself stolen the poison then Roger may be liable for handling contrary to s 22 of the Theft Act 1968. A consideration of the fourth sentence reveals two more possibilities; criminal damage to the mint under s 1(2) of the Criminal Damage Act 1971 and, more seriously, the attempted murder of Belinda contrary to s 1 of the Criminal Attempts Act 1981. The fifth, sixth and seventh sentences raise the issue of Roger's possible liability for the homicide of Jasper and criminal damage again, but this time under s 1(1) of the Criminal Damage Act 1971 in relation to Devlin the dog (although liability is unlikely to be established as Devlin probably does not 'belong to another' within the meaning of the Act. The final sentence requires a consideration of whether Roger will be liable for the homicide of the milkman; a question which involves a consideration of the rules relating to causation.

When we consider what possible defences Roger may be able to raise in relation to the offences identified above, it is important to distinguish between two different types. The first involves a denial of an element of the offence being considered, while the second type applies even when the elements of the offence have been established, but, nevertheless, the presence of special factors excuse the defendant from liability. A failure to establish causation would, in the case of a result crime, be an example of the first type while self-defence would be an example of the second type. The first type of defence will automatically be considered during stage five of our problem-solving process (see below), so all that is required here is to note any possible defences of the second kind. However, a sentence by sentence examination of the problem scenario fails to reveal defences, such as necessity, duress, self-defence etc that Roger might reasonably be able to raise.

Rebecca's liability

An examination of the scenario reveals that it is only in the second sentence that Rebecca's possible criminal liability comes into question. The obvious offence that should be noted here is, of course, a statutory conspiracy to murder contrary to s 1(1) of the Criminal Law Act 1977. In addition, her possible liability as an accomplice to murder or attempted murder under s 8 of the Accessories and Abettors Act 1861 also should be considered.

The facts of the scenario do not seem to suggest any defence that Rebecca might reasonably be able to raise. Like Roger, she will be limited to arguing that one or more of the elements that make up the respective offences are not made out. This is a matter for detailed discussion and is best left until stage five below.

Boris's liability

If we read through the scenario it becomes clear that it is the third sentence which raises issues relating to Boris's liability. As we noted when reading through the question during the second stage of the problem-solving process, the factual information provided here is insufficient as it stands to support any single argument as to Boris's liability. This being the case we have to be prepared to construct several hypothetical possibilities, each being consistent with the known facts and each entailing differing degrees of criminal liability.

- We assume that Boris does not know of Roger's intention to murder Belinda and has himself obtained the poison by lawful means. This is quite possible; Roger may have told Boris that the poison is required for some legitimate purpose such as to kill vermin or garden weeds. On this construction it seems likely that Boris will lack *mens rea* for any criminal liability.

- Alternatively, we can assume that Boris does not know of Roger's criminal purpose, but has obtained the poison illegally. The possible offences to note in these circumstances are theft contrary to s 1(1) of the Theft Act 1968 or, if

10

Boris has not stolen the poison himself, handling stolen property contrary to s 22(1) of the same Act.

- The final possibility would seem to be that Boris does know either of Roger's general intention to kill or of his specific intention to murder Belinda. In this situation his liability as an accomplice contrary to s 8 of the Accessories and Abettors Act 1861 in relation to the attempted murder of Belinda and the murder of Jasper must be considered. There is also, of course, the possibility of a statutory conspiracy contrary to s 1(1) of the Criminal Law Act 1977 and, as noted above, theft or handling if he obtained the poison illegally.

As was the case in relation to Roger and Rebecca, the facts do not reveal any defences that Boris will be able to put forward.

Belinda's liability

The information provided in the fifth and eighth sentences indicates that Belinda's actions have resulted in the death of two people; Jasper and the milkman. This being the case, her liability for homicide should be considered.

However, it seems clear from the facts, that, while no general defence appears relevant, Belinda has no mental responsibility in relation to the death of Jasper, a point to be made plain in the consideration of her liability below. It is equally clear, given the key words in sentence eight, 'trance-like state', that a plea of automatism should be considered in relation to the death of the milkman.

Once you have worked through the scenario, identifying offences and defences, as demonstrated above, you should be in possession of rough notes, similar to those illustrated in Figure 1, that can form the basis of a fully developed answer.

Figure 1 Summary of possible liability

PARTY	OFFENCE	COMMENTS	DEFENCE
Roger	Soliciting murder (s 4 OAP 1861)		
	Conspiracy to murder (s 1 CLA 1977)	With Rebecca and possibly Boris	
	Common law incitement to steal	Depends on what Roger asked Boris to do	
	Handling (s 22 TA 1968)	Depends on whether Boris acquired the poison illegally and whether Roger knew this	
	Criminal damage (s 1(2) CDA 1971)	To the mint – no need for property to belong to another for s 1(2)	
	Criminal damage (s 1(1) CDA 1971)	To the dog – probably not liable, the dog must belong to another	
	Attempted murder (s 1(1) CAA 1981)	Of Belinda	
	Murder	Of Jasper – doctrine of transferred malice and rules relating to causation relevant	
	Murder	Of milkman – doctrine of transferred malice and rules relating to causation relevant	
Rebecca	Conspiracy (s 1(1) CLA 1977)	With Roger – note Rebecca plays no part in the plan	
	Accomplice (s 8 AAA 1861)	Deliberate departure from the common plan *re* murder of Jasper, accidental departure *re* attempted murder of Belinda	

Figure 1 (continued)

PARTY	OFFENCE	COMMENTS	DEFENCE
Boris	Theft/handling (s 1(1)/s 22 TA 1968)	Depends on whether the poison has been obtained illegally	
	Accomplice (s 8 AAA 1861)	Depends on B know-ing R's purpose)	
	Conspiracy (s 1(1) CLA 1977)	Depends on B know-ing and agreeing with R's purpose	
Belinda	Homicide	Of Jasper – no *mens rea* of milkman – no *mens rea* and no *actus reus*	Automatism

(4)   Define the offences

The next task, having identified the offences that might reasonably be relevant, is to provide as precise a statutory or common law definition as is possible for each offence. It is at this stage that you can start to actually write out your answer. These definitions will then be used in the final stage of the problem-solving process as the basis for a reasoned argument as to whether or not the various offence conditions are satisfied.

(5)   Engage in legal reasoning

Roger's liability

When Roger suggests to Rebecca that they should murder his wife he incurs liability under s 4 of the Offences Against the Person Act 1861 which states that it is an offence to:

> 'Solicit, encourage, persuade or endeavour to persuade or ... propose to any person, to murder any other person.'

This is a statutory form of incitement to which the principles relating to the common law offence would seem to equally apply. The suggestion must reach the mind of the incitee (*R v Banks* (1873)) and since we are told that Rebecca 'agrees' it seems clear that this element is made out. Similarly, the requirement that the incitee must know the facts that make the incited conduct criminal is obviously satisfied as Roger suggests that they 'murder' his wife (*R v Curr* (1968)).

Rebecca must surely realise that murder involves the commission of an offence. There seems little doubt, then, that the requirements of the *actus reus* are satisfied.

 Generally, it is best to analyse the issues relating to the *actus reus* before considering those relating to the *mens rea*.

Although Roger clearly has an intention to incite, it is not so clear whether or not he also intended Rebecca to act on the incitement. The fact that she 'does nothing' is hardly relevant as far as Roger's intention is concerned. Both an intention to incite and an intention that the incitee act on the suggestion are required as part of the *mens rea* of the offence (*Invicta Plastics Ltd v Clare* (1976)). However, it seems clear that Roger does know that Rebecca knows that what is being suggested is a crime; another element of the *mens rea* (*R v Curr* (1968)). Providing Roger intends Rebecca to act on his suggestion that they murder Belinda it seems that he will be liable for soliciting murder contrary to s 4 of the Offences Against the Person Act 1861.

It is possible that when Rebecca 'agrees' with Roger that they murder Belinda, a statutory conspiracy under s 1(1) of the Criminal Law Act 1977 may occur. Section 1(1), as amended by s 5 of the Criminal Attempts Act 1981, provides that where a defendant agrees with any others:

'... that a course of conduct shall be pursued which, if the agreement is carried out in accordance with their intentions, either:

(a)   will necessarily amount to or involve the commission of any offence or offences by one or more of the parties to the agreement; or

(b)   would do so but for the existence of facts which render the offence or any of the offences impossible,

he is guilty of conspiracy to the offence or offences in question.'

Clearly, Roger has agreed with Rebecca (and possibly with Boris) on a course of conduct, killing Belinda, that if carried out would necessarily involve the commission of an offence, that of murder. Moreover, Roger's subsequent conduct in obtaining the poison, injecting it into the mint and giving it to Belinda, is evidence that at the time of the agreement with Rebecca he had an intention that the offence should actually be carried out. Roger would seem, therefore, to have satisfied both the *actus reus* and *mens rea* requirements of this offence. The fact that Rebecca and/or Boris may be acquitted of conspiracy (see below) would be no bar to Roger's conviction (s 5(8) Criminal Law Act 1977).

Next we have to consider Roger's possible liability relating to his obtaining of the poison from Boris. As has been noted, the ambiguity of the facts in relation to this aspect of the problem necessitate the consideration of various possi-

14

bilities. If Roger suggests that Boris commits a crime in order to obtain and supply the poison, possibly theft or handling, then Roger will, of course, be committing a common law incitement. The *actus reus* of incitement includes not only suggesting, encouraging, persuading, but also threatening or pressurising and Roger may well have done one or more of these actions in the course of obtaining the poison from Boris (*Race Relations Board v Applin* (1973)).

The *mens rea* requirements have been already outlined above in our discussion of the offence of soliciting murder. Assuming these requirements are satisfied, and such a construction is certainly a plausible fit with the information provided in the scenario, then Roger will be liable for inciting the theft or handling of the poison by Boris. He will not, however, he liable for the offence of incitement to conspire as this was abolished by s 5(7) of the Criminal Law Act 1977. Somewhat more arguably, Roger will also not be liable for incitement to aid, abet, procure or counsel the offence of murder as s 30(4) of the Criminal Law Act 1977 seems to assume that there is no such offence.

If the poison constitutes 'stolen goods', then Roger will most likely be liable for handling contrary to s 22(1) of the Theft Act 1968. This offence will be committed if:

'... a person handles stolen goods if (otherwise than in the course of stealing) knowingly or believing them to be stolen goods he dishonestly receives the goods, or dishonestly undertakes or assists in their retention, removal, disposal or realisation by or for the benefit of another person, or if he arranges to do so.'

The particular form of handling that Roger may have engaged in would seem to be 'receiving' and this, unlike the other forms of handling need not be 'for the benefit of another'.

By injecting poison into the mint Roger will incur liability under s 1(2) of the Criminal Damage Act 1971 as he intentionally damages property and he intends by the damage to endanger the life of another, namely Belinda. However, it is less likely that Roger will be liable for criminal damage to Devlin the dog. Section 1(1) of the Criminal Damage Act 1971 provides that:

'... a person who without lawful excuse destroys or damages any property belonging to another, intending to destroy or damage such property, or being reckless as to whether any such property would be destroyed or damaged, is guilty of an offence ...'

Although, a dog qualifies as property within the meaning of s 10(1), it is not clear whether Devlin 'belongs to another'. If we accept at face value the statement in the scenario that the dog belongs to Jasper then the requirements of the *actus reus* are made out. Alternatively, it can be argued that Devlin really belongs to Roger, rather than to the nine year old Jasper, as property will be treated as belonging to anyone having 'custody or control' of it (s 10(2) Criminal Damage Act 1971). If this is, indeed, the case, then there is no *actus reus* and, therefore, no liability.

More seriously, Roger will also become liable for the attempted murder of Belinda when he hands her the poisoned mint. Section 1(1) of the Criminal Attempts Act 1981 provides that:

'If, with intent to commit an offence to which this section applies, a person does an act which is more than merely preparatory to the commission of the offence, he is guilty of attempting to commit the offence.'

Although the phrase 'more than merely preparatory' is somewhat vague, it is submitted that since Roger has done everything necessary to kill Belinda, he has certainly gone beyond mere preparation. The 'last act' doctrine, as it was known, is no longer good law and it is clear that an attempt can now occur at an earlier stage (*R v Gullefer* (1990); *R v Jones* (1990)). However, the doctrine is still useful in that where a 'last act' has been committed, as in these circumstances, there is inevitably an act which goes beyond mere preparation. It is, therefore, a positive although not a negative guide as to whether an attempt has occurred. Clearly, Roger has the *mens rea* for the offence as it is his intention to kill Belinda.

There is, usually, little point in discussing a non-fatal offence such as administering a noxious substance contrary to s 23 of the Offences Against the Person Act 1861 when it is quite clear that the victim has died. In these circumstances one can engage directly in a consideration of liability for homicide.

 If the victim has died within a year and a day do not consider non-fatal offences, but move directly to a discussion of homicide.

There seems little doubt that Roger will be liable for the murder of Jasper. The *actus reus* of murder is causing the death of a human being and Roger, by doing 'nothing' while Jasper ate the mint, has done this. Although the criminal law does not normally impose liability for omitting to act, Roger will be culpable either on the grounds that he has, by injecting food with poison, created a dangerous situation which he has then done nothing to rectify (*R v Miller* (1983)), or that he is in breach of a parental duty of care owed to Jasper (*R v Gibbens and Procter* (1918)). The *mens rea* element of the offence, an intention to kill or cause grievous bodily harm, will be satisfied because Roger's intention to kill Belinda can be transferred to Jasper (*R v Latimer* (1886)).

Finally, Roger's possible liability for the homicide of the milkman must be considered. As was stated above, he clearly has the intention to kill Belinda and this intention to kill a human being can be transferred to the milkman, establishing the required *mens rea* for murder. However, as it seems unlikely that a court would hold the death of the milkman to be a reasonably foreseeable consequence of Roger's actions, the causation element of the *actus reus* is lacking.

Having considered Roger's liability in some detail we must now repeat this process in relation to the other parties involved in the scenario.

Rebecca's liability

When Rebecca 'agrees' with Roger that they should murder Belinda she may well be incurring liability as a party to a conspiracy to murder. A consideration of the definition of a statutory conspiracy, as provided above, indicates that Rebecca has agreed on a 'course of conduct' that if carried out will involve the commission of an offence. The *actus reus* requirements for a statutory conspiracy contrary to s 1(1) of the Criminal Law Act 1977 would, therefore, seem to be satisfied. However, the position as regards the *mens rea* is somewhat more problematic as a result of the decision of the House of Lords in *R v Anderson* (1986)). In this case Lord Bridge said that:

> '... beyond the mere fact of agreement, the necessary *mens rea* of the crime is, in my opinion, established if, and only if, it is shown that the accused, when he entered into the agreement, intended to play some part in the agreed course of conduct in furtherance of the criminal purpose which the agreed course of conduct was intended to achieve.'

If, as a straightforward reading of the scenario indicates, Rebecca has no intention to play any part in the plan to kill Belinda then, according to the above dicta, she will lack the necessary *mens rea* for conspiracy.

Notwithstanding, Lord Bridge's judgment in *Anderson*, there is authority for suggesting that a party, such as Rebecca, who does not themselves intend to play any part in carrying out the agreement, will, nevertheless be liable for conspiracy simply by agreeing that others should carry out the offence. In the Court of Appeal case of *R v Siracusa* (1989), Lord Justice O'Connor attempted to clarify Lord Bridge's comments by relocating them in the context of his speech as a whole. He commenced by casting doubt on Lord Bridge's intention to restrict liability for conspiracy to those who have an intention to play some part in the proposed offence and then went on to state that:

> '... participation in conspiracy is infinitely variable, it can be active or passive ... consent, that is the agreement or adherence to the agreement can be inferred if it is proved that he knew what was going on and intention to participate in the furtherance of the criminal purpose is also established by his failure to stop the unlawful activity.'

It seems, then, that Rebecca would have the requisite *mens rea*, consisting of an intention to play a part in the agreement to murder Belinda, such an intention being inferred from her failure to stop the unlawful activity.

By agreeing to Roger's suggestion that they murder Belinda, Rebecca is also 'counselling' ,ie encouraging the commission of the offence, and may, therefore, also be liable as an accomplice. Section 8 of the Accessories and Abettors Act 1861 provides:

17

'Whoever shall aid, abet, counsel, or procure the commission ... (of an offence) ... shall be liable to be tried, indicted and punished as a principal offender.'

The *mens rea* requirements that the defendant know the type of offence contemplated by the principal and, in the case of murder, that she foresaw that death or grievous bodily harm was a possible result of the common plan being carried out also seem to be satisfied as far as the attempted murder of Belinda is concerned (*Chan Wing Siu v R* (1985), *R v Roberts* (1993)). However, Rebecca's liability as an accomplice to the murder of Jasper will depend on whether his death was a deliberate or accidental departure from the common plan. Basically, a defendant will be liable for all the accidental or unforeseen consequences that follow from the common plan being put into operation (*R v Baldessare* (1930); *R v Betts and Ridley* (1930)). Conversely, where the principal deliberately departs from the agreed plan then the 'accomplice' is no longer a party to his actions (*Davies v DPP* (1954)). Roger's inactivity in standing by and allowing Jasper to eat the poisoned mint amounts to a deliberate departure from the common design (*R v Saunders and Archer* (1573)), particularly when one considers that he owed a parental duty of care to his son (*R v Gibbens and Proctor* (1918)) in addition to a duty to rectify the dangerous situation that he had created (*R v Miller* (1983)). Hence, it seems that while Rebecca will be an accomplice to the attempted murder of Belinda (and the criminal damage for that matter), she will not be liable in relation to the murder of Jasper.

Boris's liability

If Boris does not know of Roger's intention to murder Belinda and has himself obtained and supplied the poison lawfully, then he will not be liable for any criminal offences. On the other hand, if he has obtained the poison illegally then liability for theft, deception or handling contrary to the Theft Act 1968, whichever is appropriate, will be incurred. Moreover, if Boris knows of Roger's precise criminal purpose then by supplying the poison he will render himself liable as an accomplice to the attempted murder of Belinda. Clearly, the provision of the poison will amount to 'aiding' the commission of the offence thus satisfying the *actus reus* requirements of the offence. As far as *mens rea* is concerned, Boris will be exactly the same position as Rebecca, ie liable as an accomplice to the attempted murder of Belinda, but not liable in relation to the murder of Jasper, because, as explained above, this constitutes a deliberate departure from the common plan.

If Boris has supplied the poison knowing that Roger intends to kill someone with it, but not knowing who in particular, then it would seem that he will be liable as an accomplice in relation to both the attempted murder of Belinda and the actual murder of Jasper. This is because the offences committed all fall within the broad range within the contemplation of Boris; in short he has given Roger a 'blank cheque' as far as killing anyone is concerned (*DPP for Northern Ireland v Maxwell* (1978)).

Providing he knows of the the plan to kill Belinda it would seem that Boris would join Roger and Rebecca in the conspiracy to murder contrary to s 1 of the Criminal Law Act 1977. Note that Boris's *mens rea* here is far more certain than that of Rebecca. As we saw above, Rebecca will only be liable if the 'gloss' provided by the Court of Appeal in *Siracusa* is applied to the decision of the House of Lords in *Anderson*. Boris, because he agrees to '... play some part in the course of conduct ...' by supplying the poison, will clearly have the requisite *mens rea* even on a narrow application of the law as stated in *Anderson*.

Belinda's liability

Obviously, Belinda will have no liability as far as the death of Jasper is concerned as she lacks the *mens rea* required for any form of homicide. Although she has clearly caused the death of the milkman she will, again, lack the necessary *mens rea* either on the basis of a plea of automatism or on the grounds of insanity. It would seem that, as her 'trance-like' state has been brought about by an external event, namely, the shock of witnessing the death of her son, automatism rather than insanity will be the appropriate defence here (*R v Sullivan* (1984)).

Scenario 2

Nick, Keith and Andrew agree to 'rough up' Jones and Goss, two accountancy lecturers whom they particularly dislike. Nick is aware, but Keith is unaware that Andrew intends taking a cut-throat razor with him.

During the attack on the accountancy lecturers, Andrew punched Roy, Jones's twin brother, on the nose while Nick held him. Roy had a weak heart and died. Andrew then took out his razor and plunged it into Goss's throat crying, 'Debit that, you number cruncher!' Goss died instantly. Keith who had been present during the attack shouted repeatedly to Nick and Andrew to stop.

Discuss the criminal liability of the parties. Would your answer be different if Andrew had realised that it was Roy not Jones that he hit?

Although this question might appear at first glance to principally involve offences against the person a closer reading indicates that it is the inchoate offences and participation that pose problematic issues of central importance. Once again it is necessary to apply the procedures outlined in Chapter 1:

(1)   Read the rubric

'Discuss the criminal liability of the parties. Would your answer be different if Andrew had realised that it was Roy not Jones that he hit?'

Rather a long rubric containing that typical examiner's trick, the 'sting in the tail'. Remember to circle in red or highlight the last sentence to remind yourself to deal with this 'sting in the tail' after you have dealt with the main body of the question. You are asked to discuss the liability of the parties who in this case are Nick, Keith and Andrew.

Highlight the 'sting in the tail'.

(2) Read the scenario

Remember, if you try to work out all the legal implications during a single reading of the scenario you are likely to simply end-up being seriously confused by the sheer complexity of the interrelationship of the various legal issues involved. As you will have no doubt noticed the average criminal law tutorial always contains at least one maniacally jabbering student suffering from just this advanced state of mental 'melt down'. In order to avoid the same fate, read the scenario without worrying too much about the law. Simply, aim at an understanding of the facts, noting any areas of factual uncertainty, but avoiding any detailed legal analysis.

The facts of this particular problem might appear at first glance relatively unambiguous, but note that there is probably a 'hidden' incitement in that one of the three potential defendants must have initiated the agreement to 'rough up' the victims. Moreover, it is not clear precisely what the parties have agreed to in the first two sentences. Similarly, the fact that Nick knows that Andrew intends taking a razor with him implies that there might be a second, more serious conspiracy between these two characters. Moreover, as we shall see there are uncertainties relating to the *mens rea* requirements of several of the relevant offences.

Avoid 'tunnel vision'. Remember that both the facts and the law can be 'open-textured'.

(3) Identify the relevant offences and defences

Andrew's liability

Although Andrew is the third named party in the scenario we commence with him because it is always a good tactic when secondary liability is in issue to identify and deal with the principal offender at the outset. This procedure often considerably simplifies the discussion of the liability of the other parties involved and is a useful tip to remember.

The stated facts do not indicate which of the three parties involved was responsible for making the initial suggestion to the others that they 'rough up' Jones and Goss, but, obviously, some such suggestion must have been made by at least one of them. If it was Andrew, and it may well have been as he is the principal offender in the scenario, then his liability for a common law incitement must be considered. However, it is not clear precisely what offences he is inciting. Obviously an assault occasioning actual bodily harm as far as Keith is concerned, but possibly an incitement to do grievous bodily harm or maybe even murder was made to Nick.

The first sentence of the scenario clearly indicates the existence of a statutory conspiracy between all three parties to commit an assault occasioning actual bodily harm contrary to s 1 Criminal Law Act 1977. However, the second sentence suggests a second, more serious, conspiracy between Andrew and Nick to commit grievous bodily harm or, possibly, even murder.

Andrew's liability for the homicide of both Roy and Goss will obviously require consideration. Nevertheless, as it is not clear precisely when Roy dies (another typical examiner's trick), Andrew's liability for s 47 of the Offences Against the Person Act 1861 will also need to be discussed.

There do not seem to be any general defences that might be reasonably available to Andrew on the basis of the facts provided.

Nick's liability

As we noted in relation to Andrew, someone must have initiated the agreement by suggesting the offence. If it was in fact Nick who triggered the agreement in this way then liability for a common law incitement to carry out 'an assault occasioning actual bodily harm', contrary to s 47 of the Offences Against the Person Act 1861, will need to be considered. As we also noted above, Nick might be liable for a second conspiracy with Andrew to do grievous bodily harm or even murder.

It is possible to identify two further offences that Nick may be liable for in the third sentence. Obviously, his liability as an accomplice, under s 8 of the Accessories and Abettors Act 1861, to the assault by Andrew and for the manslaughter of Roy springs to mind, but somewhat less obviously there also appears to be a common battery and false imprisonment. In addition, it will be necessary to consider Nick's possible liability as an accomplice to the murder of Goss.

Aside from arguments concerning lack of appropriate *mens rea* the facts of the scenario do not appear to reveal any general or particular defences that Nick will be able to raise.

Keith's liability

Keith, like Nick, and, indeed, Andrew, appears to be a party to the conspiracy to rough up the accountancy lecturers. Unlike the other two, Keith's liability under s 1(1) of the Criminal Law Act 1977 does not extend to a second, more serious, conspiracy because he does not know that Andrew intends to take a razor with him. Because he agrees to the plan to attack Goss and Jones, Keith may possibly have encouraged some of the offences committed by Nick and Andrew on Roy and Goss, therefore, liability under s 8 Accessories and Abettors Act 1861 as an accomplice to manslaughter and murder should also be considered.

There do not seem to be any general defences as such that Keith will be able to raise although the question of whether or not he has made an effective withdrawal will have to be examined. In addition, his defence would also draw attention to the point that mere presence at the scene of a crime is insufficient to found liability as an accomplice.

Having identified all the offences that the three parties might possibly have committed you should be in a position to create an outline answer plan somewhat similar to that contained in Figure 2.

Figure 2   Summary of possible liability

PARTY	OFFENCE	COMMENTS	DEFENCE
Andrew	Incitement	Possibly two separate offences	
	Conspiracy (s 1(1) CLA 1977	Again two possible offences	
	Assault occasioning actual bodily harm (s 47 OAP 1861)		
	Manslaughter (of Roy)	Uncertain when Roy dies – year and a day rule	
	Murder (of Goss)		
Nick	Incitement	Depends if Nick suggests any offences	
	Conspiracy (s 1(1) CLA 1977	Possibly two conspiracies	
	Accomplice (s 8 AAA 1861)	Possibly accomplice to s 47 OAP 1861 and to manslaughter of Roy and murder of Goss.	
	False imprisonment		
	Battery	ie he 'held' Roy	
Keith	Conspiracy (s 1(1) CLA 1977		
	Accomplice (s 8 AAA 1861)	Possibly accomplice to manslaughter and murder	

(4) Define the relevant offences

Remember to provide accurate definitions for each offence before going on to argue whether or not their requirements are satisfied. The importance of being able to state offence definitions accurately cannot be over-emphasised; they form the foundation upon which subsequent argument is constructed. Unfortunately, too many students fail to devote enough time and energy to the sheer hard work of learning these definitions with the regrettable result that the structure of their argument is often condemned as fundamentally unsound by ever-vigilant criminal law examiners.

 Learn all the offence definitions relevant to your syllabus.

(5) Engage in legal reasoning

Andrew's liability

As Andrew is the principal offender in this scenario it is not beyond the bounds of possibility that he initiated the agreement between the parties by suggesting that they 'rough up' Jones and Goss. If this is, indeed, the case then it seems that he will be liable for a common law incitement to commit an assault. Assuming that Andrew does initiate the agreement it would seem clear that the central conduct of the *actus reus*, '... to urge or spur on by advice, encouragement or persuasion ...' (*per* Lord Denning in *Race Relations Board v Applin* (1973)) is present. The second element of the *actus reus*; that the incitement reach the mind of the incitee, is obviously satisfied as we are told that Nick and Keith 'agree' (*R v Banks* (1873)). The third and final requirement of the *actus reus* also seems to be present as the incitee must surely know that 'roughing up' someone involves the commission of an offence (*R v Curr* (1968)). There are also three elements that need to be satisfied in order to establish the *mens rea* of incitement: that the incitor intends to incite, an intention that the incitee act on the incitement (*Invicta Plastics Ltd v Clare* (1976)) and, finally, that the incitor knows or believes that the incitee knows or believes that what is being suggested is a crime (*R v Curr* (1968)). All these elements would seem to be satisfied on the basis of the facts of the scenario.

It is quite possible to present a reasonable argument to the effect that there may be a second incitement to do grievous bodily harm or even murder. Since we are told that Nick knows that Andrew intends to take a razor with him it is not unreasonable to suppose that Andrew has himself revealed this in the process of making an explicit or implicit suggestion that they cause grievous bodily harm or death. If this is, indeed, the case, then, all the elements of the *actus reus* and *mens rea*, considered above, would seem to be present.

Because Andrew, Nick and Keith 'agree' to 'rough up' the accountancy lecturers there is the possibility of a statutory conspiracy to commit at least an assault offence contrary to the Criminal Law Act 1977. However, adopting the same line of argument that we developed in relation to incitement, there may also be a second conspiracy between Andrew and Nick to commit either grievous bodily harm or even murder. This would depend of whether or not there actually was an agreement between Andrew and Nick to commit either of these offences. The fact that Nick knows that Andrew intends taking the razor with him tends to suggest that there was. However, merely discussing the possibility of committing an offence will not amount to an agreement to commit it (*R v O'Brien* (1974)).

Section 1(1) of the Criminal Law Act 1977, as amended by s 5 of the Criminal Attempts Act 1981, provides that it is an offence to agree on a:

'... course of conduct ... which either:

(a) will necessarily amount to or involve the commission of any offence ...; or

(b) would do so but for the existence of facts which render the commission of the offence ... impossible.'

Obviously, in agreeing to 'rough up' Jones and Goss the parties have agreed on a course of conduct that will necessarily involve the commission of an offence and, therefore, fall within s 1(1)(a). If there is, indeed, an additional agreement between Andrew and Nick to do grievous bodily harm or murder, then, there will be a second conspiracy to commit the relevant offence. The *mens rea* requirements would seem to be satisfied in relation to both of these possible conspiracies. Andrew, clearly, has an intention to agree in both cases. Moreover, he would seem to have either the requisite *mens rea* as specified by the Court of Appeal in *R v Siracusa* (1989), ie an intention that the offence be carried out, or that posited by the House of Lords in *R v Anderson* (1986), ie an intention to play some part in the agreed course of conduct.

Andrew's action in punching Roy on the nose raises the possibility of liability for an '... assault occasioning actual bodily harm ...' contrary to s 47 of the Offences Against the Person Act 1861. Although we are told that Roy subsequently dies, this non-fatal offence still requires consideration because the death may have occurred after 'a year and a day' and, therefore, would not constitute the *actus reus* of homicide (*R v Dyson* (1908)). The *actus reus* of the s 47 offence consists of three elements: an 'assault' in either a narrow sense of causing the victim to apprehend immediate physical violence or in the wider sense of direct physical contact; 'occasioning' which implies causation and 'actual bodily harm'; that is, any hurt or injury likely to interfere with health or comfort (*R v Miller* (1954)). These three elements all appear to be satisfied; as Andrew punches Roy there is clearly an 'assault', in the wider sense, which must surely have caused an interference with health or, at the very least, comfort. The *mens rea* requirements for this offence are an intention or recklessness in relation to the initial assault, but not necessarily in relation to the resulting actual bodily harm (*R v Savage* (1991)). Andrew might argue that he did not have such an intention to assault *Roy*, but, rather, an intention to assault *Jones*. However, this line of argument can be countered by reference to the doctrine of transferred malice; that is, the intention to assault Jones is transferred to Roy (*R v Latimer* (1886)).

If Roy dies within a year and a day, Andrew's liability for homicide will have to be considered. The *actus reus* of all forms of homicide is the same and consists of two elements; causation, and the requirement that the death occurs within the specified period of a year and a day. As regards causation, the information provided in the scenario is ambiguous; Roy's heart attack might be entirely unrelated to the assault, in which case Andrew will not have caused the death (*R v White* (1910)). Alternatively, if the assault precipitates the heart attack, Andrew will have caused the death, notwithstanding the fact that Roy suffers from a pre-existing heart condition which renders him especially vulnerable (*R v Blaue* (1975)). Assuming that Roy does, indeed, die with a year and a day, then, subject to the previous comments about causation, the *actus reus* of homicide would be established.

If the scenario includes a death always question whether it has occurred within a year and a day.

Andrew would almost certainly not be liable for murder in relation to the death of Roy, because it is extremely unlikely that he had the necessary *mens rea*, ie an intention to kill or cause grievous bodily harm, at the moment when he struck the fatal blow. This being the case, his liability for involuntary manslaughter must be considered. Unfortunately, following the case of *R v Prentice and Others* (1993)), there seems to be some uncertainty concerning the appropriate form of *mens rea* for this offence. If *Prentice* is given a broad interpretation it would seem that all incidents of involuntary manslaughter, with the exception of 'motor manslaughter' and 'constructive manslaughter' should be considered as cases of killing by gross negligence. However, it may be that the decision of the Court of Appeal in *Prentice* will be given a narrower interpretation which restricts its effect to 'breach of duty' cases. In the somewhat unlikely event of this latter interpretation being adopted, then reckless killing should also be considered.

In relation to killing by gross negligence it may well be that Andrew does have the requisite *mens rea* in that punching someone on the nose, in the circumstances of this case, probably would constitute a major deviation from the standards of the reasonable person (*Bateman* (1925)). This is because the gross negligence need not relate to a risk of death or even serious injury, but merely a risk of *injury to health* (*R v Stone and Dobinson* (1977)). After all, surely a reasonable person would have thought of the risk of some injury to health resulting from such an inherently unreasonable action?

If, notwithstanding the decision in *Prentice*, reckless killing is still a relevant form of manslaughter to consider, then it seems clear that Andrew is reckless in the *Caldwell* sense. *Caldwell* recklessness can be usefully summarised as the conscious or unconscious taking of an obvious risk (*MPC v Caldwell* (1982)). Although the House of Lords in the case of *R v Reid* (1992) stated that, in appropriate circumstances, the court might be prepared to give the phrase 'obvious risk' a subjective meaning, the facts of this case clearly fall outside the type of exceptional situations contemplated by their lordships. Almost certainly 'obvious risk' will be given the meaning of objectively obvious; that is obvious to the reasonable person and, adopting the line of argument developed in relation to killing by gross negligence, it may well be that a reasonable person would appreciate a significant risk of serious harm, although probably not death, resulting from a blow on the nose. If the aforementioned argument that there is an obvious risk is accepted, then, it seems clear that Andrew either consciously or unconsciously takes that risk and is, therefore, reckless in the *Caldwell* sense. Certainly, there seems no scope for the so called 'loophole' argument in relation to *Caldwell* recklessness on the facts of this case; Andrew can hardly have foreseen the risk of death or serious harm following the punch on the nose and then have concluded that there was no risk at all (*Chief Constable of Avon and Somerset Constabulary v Shimmen* (1986); *R v Reid* (1992)).

Perhaps the most appropriate form of homicide to consider in relation to the facts of this scenario would be constructive manslaughter, or, as it is sometimes known, the illegal act doctrine. There are three elements to the *actus reus* of this offence; there must be a dangerous, criminal act which causes death. However, it is the *mens rea* requirement which renders this type of involuntary manslaughter particularly relevant to the scenario under consideration. This is because all that is required is an intention to do an act which is in fact unlawful and dangerous and which causes death, it is not necessary to prove that the defendant had known that the act was unlawful or dangerous (*DPP v Newbury and Jones* (1976)).

Two of the *actus reus* requirements are unproblematic. There is, obviously, a criminal action in that, as discussed above, the punch on the nose would constitute an offence contrary to s 47 of the Offences Against the Person Act 1861 (*R v Arobieke* (1988)). In addition to being criminal it would also seem to be a 'dangerous' act in that a reasonable person would foresee some physical harm resulting from it (*R v Church* (1966)). The causation element is somewhat more problematic in that it is not clear whether or not the death is related to the blow at all (*R v White* (1910)). However, as we have already noted above, if the blow precipitates a heart attack then Andrew will have caused the death notwithstanding the fact that Roy suffers from a pre-existing heart condition that renders him particularly vulnerable (*R v Blaue* (1975)).

The *mens rea* requirement for constructive manslaughter seems relatively straightforward as it seems clear that Andrew has an intention to do an action, ie the punch on the nose, which is in fact both criminal and dangerous.

To summarise, then, it seems virtually certain that Andrew would be liable for constructive manslaughter, alternatively he would probably be liable for killing by gross negligence.

Andrew's liability for the murder of Goss is clearly unproblematic; obviously he satisfies both the *actus reus* and *mens rea* requirements. Clearly, he has caused the death of a human-being within a year and a day and, equally clearly, he has an intention to kill, or, at the very least, an intention to cause grievous bodily harm.

There seem to be no general defences that would be available to Andrew in the situation described in the scenario.

Nick's liability

If it is Nick who initiates the agreement to 'rough up' the accountancy lecturers then he will be liable for a common law incitement. We have already discussed the *actus reus* and *mens rea* conditions for this offence in relation to Andrew and the same considerations would apply to Nick. Similarly, in the course of our discussion of Andrew's liability, we pointed out that not only would Nick be liable for a conspiracy to do actual bodily harm, but also that there was a possibility of a second more serious conspiracy to cause grievous bodily harm or even murder.

In holding Roy, Nick would not only commit a battery, but also the common law offence of false imprisonment. The *actus reus* of battery is defined in *Cole v Turner* (1705) as the least touching of another in anger. Clearly, in holding Roy so that Andrew could hit him, Nick will have satisfied this requirement. Moreover, as there seems to be no doubt that he intended to hold Roy, Nick would also have the *mens rea* for battery which is either intention or recklessness (*R v Venna* (1976)). False imprisonment can be defined as intentionally or recklessly restraining the victim's freedom of movement. All the elements of this offence seem to be satisfied as there is an intentional unlawful restraint. The fact that the imprisonment is only momentary and does not involve a confinement in a building will not absolve Nick of liability (*Ludlow v Burgess* (1971)).

Nick's liability as an accomplice to Andrew in relation to the s 47 assault, the manslaughter of Roy and the murder of Goss will all need to be considered. Secondary liability arises under the Accessories and Abettors Act 1861, s 8 of which provides that:

> 'Whosoever shall aid, abet, counsel, or procure ... the commission of an offence ... shall be liable to be tried, indicted, and punished as a principal offender.'

Nick, by holding Roy, would clearly seem to satisfy the *actus reus* requirement of 'aiding' Andrew, at least in relation to the first two offences. Moreover, as the s 47 offence is obviously of a similar type of offence to those contemplated by Nick when he agrees to 'rough up' Jones and Goss, the necessary *mens rea* would also be present (*R v Bainbridge* (1960)). The fact that Andrew mistakenly punches Jones's twin brother, Roy, would constitute an accidental departure from the common plan and, as such, would not absolve Nick of secondary liability (*R v Baldessare* (1930)). Similarly, Roy's death would constitute another such accidental departure from the common plan for which Nick would be liable according to the above principle.

In relation to secondary liability, always compare what the parties contemplated with what actually happened in order to establish whether or not there has been a departure from the 'common plan'.

The position is somewhat more problematic in relation to Nick's liability as an accomplice to the murder of Goss. The *actus reus* would now seem to consist of 'counselling' in that by agreeing to 'rough up' the accountancy lecturers, Nick would inevitably encourage Andrew to carry out the attack. However, it is not entirely clear as to precisely what Nick understood by this, but as he knew that Andrew intended taking a razor with him it is reasonable to assume that he realised that it might be used. If this was, indeed, the case then he could satisfy the required *mens rea* for an accomplice to murder as laid down in the Privy Council case of *R v Chan Wing-siu* (1985). In this case it was held that it was sufficient that the accomplice foresaw death or grievous bodily harm as a possible consequence of the common plan being carried out, a principle which is now of binding authority (*R v Hyde* (1990); *R v Roberts* (1993)).

It is possible, although rather unlikely, that Nick would contemplate a razor being used without also foreseeing the possibility of at least grievous bodily harm. In short, if Nick merely contemplated an attack that fell short of death or grievous bodily harm then he would not be liable as an accomplice to the murder of Goss. Indeed, the murder of Goss would, in these circumstances constitute a deliberate departure from the common plan that would have the effect of exempting Nick from liability (*Davies v DPP* (1954)). Alternatively, if, as seems more likely, Nick did foresee the possibility of death or grievous bodily harm as a consequence of the plan to attack Jones and Goss, then he would be liable as an accomplice to the murder. The killing of Goss would be within the common plan, if the possibility of death had been foreseen, or an accidental departure from it, if only the possibility of grievous bodily harm had been foreseen. In either circumstance Nick would still incur liability as a secondary liability.

Keith's liability

We have already considered the *actus reus* and *mens rea* requirements of conspiracy in our discussion of Andrew's liability and these considerations will also largely apply to Keith. However, there are two important differences in relation to Keith's liability that should be taken into consideration. Firstly, as he is unaware that Andrew intends taking a razor with him, Keith's liability for conspiracy, unlike that of Andrew and Nick, appears to be confined to the initial agreement to 'rough up' the accountancy lecturers. Secondly, it is possible, although rather unlikely, that Keith did not intend to play a part in the agreed course of conduct, and, thus, lacks the requisite *mens rea* as specified by Lord Bridge in *R v Anderson* (1986). However, the Court of Appeal in *R v Siracusa* (1989) attempted to clarify Lord Bridge's comments by relocating them in the context of his judgment as a whole. When read in this way it was said that his Lordship had not meant that the *mens rea* of conspiracy was limited to an intention to play a part in executing the agreement, but simply that when the defendant agreed to the course of conduct he knew that it involved the commission of an offence. According to this interpretation of *Anderson*, Keith would certainly have the requisite *mens rea* since he surely realised that an agreement to 'rough up' someone would involve the commission of an offence.

Keith's mere presence at the scene of the crime will be insufficient to establish the necessary *actus reus* for liability as an accomplice contrary to s 8 Accessories and Abettors Act 1861 (*R v Coney* (1881); *R v Clarkson* (1971)). Nevertheless, as we noted in relation to Nick, it can be argued that by agreeing to 'rough up' Jones and Goss, Keith must surely also encourage Andrew to engage in this course of action. As counselling the commission of an offence involves advising, encouraging, persuading, instructing, pressurising, or even threatening the principal into committing the offence, it would seem that Keith has satisfied the *actus reus* requirement for secondary liability. Keith's liability as an accomplice to the s 47 assault seems relatively unproblematic as he knows the type of offence contemplated by Andrew (*R v Bainbridge* (1960)). Moreover, as we noted in relation to Nick's liability, the manslaughter of Roy constitutes an accidental departure from the common plan for which Keith would be liable as an accomplice. In contrast, the murder of Goss constitutes a deliberate departure from the common plan, provided, of course, that Keith did not foresee the possibility of death or grievous bodily harm, and as such would exempt Keith from secondary liability in respect of this offence (*Davies v DPP* (1954)).

It seems very unlikely, merely by shouting repeatedly to Andrew and Nick to stop, that Keith has made an 'effective withdrawal' from the common plan. In these circumstances, where the defendants are actually about the business of committing the crime, it would seem that nothing short of physical intervention is likely to prove sufficient to constitute an effective withdrawal (*R v Becerra* (1975)).

The 'sting in the tail'

It is now necessary to re-evaluate the liability of the parties assuming that Andrew knew that it was Roy not Jones that he punched on the nose. This change of circumstance would not affect the liability of Andrew at all. As we have already seen, he will be liable for the assault and manslaughter of Roy in any case as a consequence of the application of the doctrine of transferred malice.

As regards Nick and Keith, the 'sting in the tail' would make a difference in that the assault on Roy now constitutes a deliberate departure from the common plan by Andrew. They will not, therefore, be liable as accomplices to either the assault or the manslaughter of Roy (*R v Saunders and Archer* (1537)).

Offences Against The Person 3

In this chapter, although the problem scenarios are once again eclectic in nature, involving several different areas of criminal liability, our intention is to focus predominately on fatal and non-fatal offences against the person. These offences cover a wide-range from minor assaults at one end of the continuum to murder at the other. The appropriate offence in relation to specific incidents in the scenarios will depend both on the degree of harm caused and the nature of the accompanying *mens rea*. However, those devious criminal law examiners are fond of producing fact situations that are 'open-textured' in relation to one or other of these elements in the hope of confusing the unsuspecting student. This being the case, you will have often to be prepared to construct alternative arguments encompassing different offences.

You may find it helpful to quickly read over the concise notes on general principles and offences against the person in Chapter 8 before considering the following scenarios.

Scenario 3

Marnah was driving one afternoon when she felt increasingly drowsy. She fell asleep and her car mounted the pavement and crashed into a wall trapping Bronwen, a pedestrian, and seriously injuring her. The crash woke Marnah who, seeing the trapped Bronwen, an old enemy, decided not to move the car. After some time, she decided that Bronwen had had enough and drove away. Jan, a passing law lecturer, witnessed the event and was very upset by the occurrence. In her efforts to erase the memory of the injured Bronwen, Jan drank a large quantity of brandy and became very drunk. She stumbled into the college where she worked and without realising dropped a lighted cigarette on the library carpet. The college caught fire and two of the students were killed in the blaze. Jan escaped, but witnessing these events drove her mad. She became convinced that her Head of Department was the Devil and killed him.

Discuss the criminal liability of Marnah and Jan.

This scenario is quite complex involving automatism, insanity and criminal damage in addition to the fatal and non-fatal offences against the person. The obvious possibility of Marnah having committed various road traffic offences will not be discussed because, with the exception of motor manslaughter and causing death by dangerous driving, most undergraduate criminal law courses do not include these offences on the syllabus.

31

Know the scope of your syllabus and restrict your discussion to the offences encompassed within it.

(1)   Read the rubric

'Discuss the criminal liability of Marnah and Jan.'

A relatively straightforward rubric without a 'sting in the tail' to complicate matters.

(2)   Read the scenario

Remember, it is important at this stage to try not to worry too much about the legal complications, simply try to obtain an overview of the facts contained in the scenario. Inevitably, some legal issues cannot fail to strike you on this initial reading; in this case the obvious examples are the possible defences of intoxication and insanity. However, experience indicates that the somewhat dubious pleasure of marking examination papers is rendered even more problematic when students insist on putting defences before offences, merge *actus reus* and *mens rea* issues and fail to clearly identify the particular offence they are considering. It is vitally important, therefore, that you keep a cool head and stick strictly to the problem-solving procedure contained in this book and, thus, hopefully, avoid unnecessary confusion both in your mind and that of the examiner.

(3)   Identify the relevant offences and defences

Marnah's liability

As we have already noted, driving offences, with the exception of motor manslaughter and causing death by dangerous driving, do not appear on most undergraduate criminal law syllabuses. If we ignore, therefore, any possible road traffic offences, Marnah's liability would commence in the second sentence when she crashes into the wall, trapping Bronwen and seriously injuring her. The relevant offences here are criminal damage to both the wall and car under s 1(1) and s 1(2), respectively, of the Criminal Damage Act 1971. Of course, there is also maliciously wounding or inflicting grievous bodily harm contrary to s 20 of the Offences Against the Person Act 1861 in relation to the injuries sustained by Bronwen. When Marnah awakes and decides not to move the car her liability for s 18 of the Offences Against the Person Act 1861 and the common law offence of false imprisonment also comes into question. Alternatively, if a lesser degree of harm is caused by keeping Bronwen trapped, then occasioning actual bodily harm contrary to s 47 of the Offences Against the Persons Act 1861 becomes relevant.

We are informed that Bronwen is 'seriously injured', but we do not know whether or not she dies as a result of these injuries. As the facts are 'open' in this respect we should also consider Marnah's possible liability in the unfortunate event of Bronwen's demise within a year and a day.

 If you are informed that someone has been 'seriously injured' always consider the possibility of the victim dying within a year and a day, thus, raising the possibility of homicide.

As she was asleep when the car first crashed into Bronwen and the wall, the defence of automatism will be of obvious relevance to this problem.

Jan's liability

We are informed that Jan became 'very drunk' and although, mercifully, this is not an offence in itself it might suggest other possible offences, such as drunk and disorderly and driving with an excess of alcohol in the bloodstream. However, not only is there no direct evidence in the scenario for these offences, but also they are not normally included in undergraduate criminal law courses. Assuming this to be case, the discussion of Jan's liability would commence in relation to criminal damage to the library and the homicide of the students. Finally, of course, Jan's liability for the murder of her Head of Department should be considered.

The defences of intoxication, automatism, diminished responsibility and insanity will all require consideration when assessing Jan's possible liability.

Figure 3 Summary of possible liability

PARTY	OFFENCE	COMMENTS	DEFENCE
Marnah	Wounding/GBH (s 20 OAP 1861)	No intention for s 18 OAP 1861	Automatism
	Criminal damage (s 1(1) CDA 1971)	To the wall	Automatism
	Criminal damage (s 1(2) CDA 1971)	To the car	Automatism
	False imprisonment		
	Wounding/GBH with intent (s 18 OAP 1861)	Must be fresh wound or additional GBH	
	Wounding/GBH (s 20 OAP 1861)	Alternative to above if no intention to do GBH	
	Assault occasioning ABH (s 47 OAP 1861)	Alternative to above if lesser degree of harm	
	Homicide	If Bronwen dies	
Jan	Criminal damage (s 1(1) or s1(2) CDA 1971	To college	Intoxication Automatism
	Section 1(3) CDA 1971	To college	Intoxication Automatism
	Homicide (manslaughter)	Of the students	Intoxication Automatism
	Homicide (murder/manslaughter)	Of Head of Department	Automatism Insanity Diminished responsibility

(4)   Define the relevant offences

Before presenting your argument as to whether or not the various elements of the *actus reus* and *mens rea* are satisfied in relation to each of the offences identified above, it is vitally important, as we have already emphasised, to provide accurate definitions for these offences. Each definition must then be analysed into *actus reus* and *mens rea*. Remember an easy way of finding the *actus reus* is to subtract any 'mental' concepts, such as, 'intentionally', 'knowingly', 'dishonestly', 'maliciously', 'recklessly', etc, from the definition. The *actus reus* and *mens rea* will then need to be sub-divided into their constituent elements which may, in turn, require further definition depending on whether that particular concept is problematic in relation to the facts of the scenario.

(5)   Engage in legal reasoning

Marnah's liability

Marnah's action in crashing into the wall, trapping Bronwen and seriously injuring her, raises questions concerning her liability under the Criminal Damage Act 1971 and the Offences Against the Person Act 1861. There may be liability under s 1(1) of the Criminal Damage Act 1971 if, as seems likely, she has damaged the wall. This offence is defined as destroying or damaging '... any property belonging to another intending to destroy or damage any such property or being reckless as to whether any such property would be destroyed or damaged ...' The *actus reus* of the offence, therefore, consists of destroying or damaging property belonging to another. It would seem extremely probable that Marnah has damaged the wall in some way as we are informed that she crashed into it. Moreover, not only would the wall fall within the s 10 (1) definition of 'property', as it is clearly of a tangible nature, but also it would belong to another (unless, of course, Marnah crashed into her own wall, perhaps at the commencement or termination of her journey).

Although, it would seem that all the requisite elements of the *actus reus* have been established, it could still be argued that because Marnah was asleep at the time of the crash there was no conscious willed action on which to found the *actus reus*. However, the plea of automatism would be unlikely to succeed in relation to the facts of this case. Since Marnah continued to drive despite feeling increasingly drowsy, it appears that she has been at fault in bringing about the state of automatism on which she is seeking to rely. In these circumstances, at least in relation to a crime of basic intent like criminal damage, she would not be allowed to succeed with the plea of automatism (*Kay v Butterworth* (1945); *R v Bailey* (1983)).

As can be seen from the definition of s 1(1) of the Criminal Damage Act 1971 the *mens rea* consists of either an intention to destroy or damage property belonging to another or being reckless as to whether any such property would be destroyed or damaged. Clearly, because she is asleep at the relevant time, Marnah would lack the requisite intention for this offence. Our discussion of her possible liability must, therefore, focus on the concept of recklessness, and, in relation to criminal damage, this means *Caldwell* recklessness (*MPC v Caldwell* (1982)). The definition of *Caldwell* recklessness, the conscious or unconscious taking of an obvious risk, must now be applied to the particular situation under consideration. Marnah's action of falling to sleep at the wheel of her car, in the absence of any sudden illness, does not seem to be of a type that their Lordships had in mind in the case of *R v Reid* (1992) as justifying a subjective interpretation of the phrase 'obvious risk'. It would appear that there is an objectively obvious risk in that a reasonable person would have surely appreciated that there was a serious risk of damaging property in continuing to drive whilst feeling increasingly drowsy (*Elliot v C* (1983)). Not only does there appear to be an obvious risk, it also seems relatively certain that Marnah consciously or unconsciously took that risk. After all, Marnah can hardly have considered the risk of damaging property by continuing to drive in an increasingly drowsy state and concluded that there was *no risk at all* (*Chief Constable of Avon and Somerset v Shimmen* (1986)). There seems no scope, therefore, for the so-called 'lacuna' argument in relation to this particular fact situation. Either Marnah did consider the risk of damaging property and decided to run that risk, or, as is, perhaps, more likely, simply failed to consider such a risk at all.

In addition, we should consider Marnah's possible liability in relation to s 1(2) of the Criminal Damage Act 1971 which is the offence of damaging or destroying property with either an intention to endanger life, or being reckless as to whether life is endangered. For this offence, unlike s 1(1), the property need not belong to another, and as it is almost certain that Marnah has damaged her car in crashing into the wall the *actus reus* would appear to be made out. As Marnah is asleep there can be no question of her having an intention to endanger life so once again her liability will depend upon a consideration of whether or not she has been reckless in the *Caldwell* sense. However, it is vitally important to appreciate that the recklessness required in relation to s 1(2) relates to something different from the recklessness required in relation to s 1(1). For s 1(2) the recklessness must refer to the conscious or unconscious taking of an obvious risk that property will be damaged and that the damaged property might endanger life (*R v Steer* (1988)). Adopting the objective interpretation of obvious risk, it does, indeed, seem that a reasonable person would have foreseen a serious risk that an increasingly drowsy driver might damage her car and that the damaged car might in turn endanger life. Once again, there is little scope for the 'lacuna' argument so it would appear that Marnah must have consciously, or, perhaps more probably, unconsciously taken such a risk.

The defence argument concerning automatism could be raised in relation to the s 1(2) as well as the s 1(1) offence, but, needless to say, it would be hardly likely to succeed for the same reasons as mentioned above.

Bronwen is seriously injured, and as Marnah obviously lacks an intention to cause grievous bodily harm the appropriate offence would be '... malicious wounding ...' or '... maliciously inflicting grievous bodily harm ...' contrary to s 20 of the Offences Against the Person Act 1861. Once the mental concept 'malicious' has been subtracted from the definition it becomes clear that the *actus reus* consists of three concepts: infliction and either a wound or grievous bodily harm. Although the concept of 'infliction' has been the subject of much case law concerning whether or not it implies an assault, it now seems settled that there is no such necessary implication (*R v Wilson* (1983)). This being the case it appears that the word 'inflicts' indicates little more than the need to establish causation. On the basis of the facts provided in the scenario, all the elements of the *actus reus* appear unproblematic; since Marnah has obviously caused Bronwen grievous bodily harm.

The *mens rea* for the s 20 offence is 'maliciously', a concept which has been interpreted to mean recklessly in the *R v Cunningham* (1957) sense of the conscious taking of an unjustified risk. Once again, it is crucial to specify the precise nature of the risk to which the offence definition relates. In *R v Mowatt* (1967), Diplock LJ placed a 'gloss' on the definition of Cunningham recklessness in relation to s 20 of the Offences Against the Person Act 1861 by stating that:

'It is quite unnecessary that the accused should have foreseen that his unlawful act might cause physical harm of the gravity described in the section, ie, a wound or serious physical injury. It is enough that he should have foreseen that some physical harm to some person, albeit of a minor character, might result.'

It seems safe to assume that the risk of some physical harm was an unjustified one in that a reasonable person would not have continued to drive whilst feeling increasingly drowsy. All that remains to be established is that Marnah actually foresaw the unjustified risk of some physical harm. The facts provided in the scenario are 'open' in this respect although it would seem odd if a driver who felt increasingly drowsy did not think, albeit fleetingly, about the possibility of crashing and causing physical harm.

When Marnah awakes and decides not to move the car liability in relation to both the common law offence of false imprisonment and s 18 of the Offences Against the Person Act 1861 becomes relevant. False imprisonment consists of the intentional or reckless unlawful restraint of the victim's freedom of movement from a particular place. Obviously, the *actus reus* requirements appear to be satisfied as Bronwen is trapped for 'some time' and since Marnah 'decides' on this course of action it seems equally obvious that she has the necessary intent.

Any attempt to deny the existence of the *actus reus* on the grounds of an omission argument that Marnah had done nothing could be countered by asserting that by continuing to drive whilst feeling increasingly drowsy she created a dangerous situation which she then had a common law duty to rectify or militate (*R v Miller* (1983)). Alternatively, it could be argued that there was a continuing act rather than a pure omission and that Marnah formed the requisite *mens rea* at some point during its continuance (*Fagan v MPC* (1969)).

Section 18 of the Offences Against the Person Act 1861 may be defined as maliciously wounding or causing grievous bodily harm with intent to do grievous bodily harm. The *actus reus* is, therefore, the same as that for s 20 and consists of proof of causation and either a wound or grievous bodily harm.

Although the scenario states that Bronwen suffered serious injuries, these seem to have occurred as a result of the initial impact and, as we have already argued, constitute the *actus reus* of the s 20 offence. In order to establish the *actus reus* of the s 18 offence it would be necessary to prove an additional wound or additional grievous bodily harm. Yet again, the facts of the scenario are 'open' in this respect. However, it is not unreasonable to suppose that trapping an already seriously injured person for 'some time' would produce just such additional injuries. Of course, any fresh injuries would have to amount to either a wound, ie, a break in all the layers of the skin (*JCC v Eisenhower* (1984)), or a serious injury (*R v Saunders* (1985)).

The *mens rea* for the s 18 offence seems unproblematic in that in deciding to keep an already seriously injured Bronwen trapped for some time, Marnah must surely have formed the requisite intent to cause serious harm. The fact that Bronwen is recognised as 'an old enemy' would tend to support the argument that Marnah did, indeed, form such an intention.

Of course, the omission argument that we noted in relation to the offence of false imprisonment could also be raised in relation to the s 18 offence and, indeed, the s 20 and s 47 offences, considered below, but it is unlikely to succeed for the same reasons.

Marnah would become liable for a second offence contrary to s 20 of the Offences Against the Person Act 1861 if by keeping Bronwen trapped she causes an additional wound or grievous bodily harm, but lacks the intention to cause grievous bodily harm necessary for the more serious s 18 offence. In these rather unlikely circumstances, Marnah would, almost certainly have the requisite *mens rea* of *Cunningham* recklessness for the s 20 offence as she must have foreseen the possibility of causing Bronwen at least some physical harm by keeping her trapped against the wall for 'some time'.

If no new wound or serious harm can be proved, or if the prosecution are unable to establish that Marnah did foresee the possibility of some physical harm, then, liability in relation to s 47 of the Offences Against the Person Act 1861 should be considered. This offence may be defined as the intentional or reckless infliction of an '... assault occasioning actual bodily harm ...' The 'assault' on which liability for s 47 is based can be either an assault in the narrow sense or in the broader sense of a battery. Since Marnah kept Bronwen trapped against the wall by a car there would clearly seem to be an assault in the broader sense of the least touching of another (*Cole v Turner* (1705)). Moreover, it is difficult to imagine how this assault could possibly fail to occasion actual bodily harm in the sense of any hurt or injury likely to interfere with the health or comfort of the victim (*R v Miller* (1954)). The *mens rea* requirement of intention or recklessness need only relate to the initial assault and this also seems unproblematic as Marnah intended to maintain the unlawful physical contact by the car (*R v Savage* (1991)).

If Bronwen died within a year and a day Marnah could become liable for either murder or manslaughter. Since the *mens rea* for murder consists of an intention to kill or cause grievous bodily harm, liability for this offence would depend on whether Marnah did form an intention to cause grievous bodily harm when she decided to keep Bronwen trapped against the wall. In the rather unlikely event that Marnah did not form such an intention then liability for various forms of involuntary manslaughter including motor manslaughter and causing death by dangerous driving as well as constructive manslaughter and killing by gross negligence could be considered. As Bronwen's death is only an implicit possibility, a detailed consideration of all these offences is not justified by the facts of the scenario. All that need be done in this regard is to very briefly indicate whether the necessary *mens rea* for any of these homicide offences is likely to be made out.

Not only does Marnah's conduct appear to amount to the gross negligence required for both killing by gross negligence and causing death by dangerous driving, but also she seems to have the requisite *Caldwell* recklessness in relation to motor manslaughter. Additionally, by deciding to keep Bronwen trapped against the wall, Marnah surely has an intention to do a dangerous and criminal act.

Jan's liability

Obviously, there should be a discussion of Jan's possible liability for criminal damage in relation to the structure and contents of the college. Section 1(3) of the Criminal Damage Act 1971 provides: 'An offence committed under this section by destroying or damaging property by fire shall be charged as arson.' Since this provision is mandatory, 'shall be charged as arson', Jan's liability would, therefore, be under either s 1(1) and (3), or under s 1(2) and (3).

The 'basic' offence of criminal damage under s 1(1) and (3) consists of intentionally or recklessly destroying or damaging property belonging to another by fire. All the elements of the *actus reus* appear to be satisfied; the college both belonged to another and constituted property and it must have suffered some damage by fire as there was a 'blaze'.

As Jan did not intend to destroy or damage the college by fire, her liability would depend on whether or not the *mens rea* of recklessness could be established. The relevant type of recklessness for criminal damage is *Caldwell* recklessness, that is the conscious or unconscious taking of an obvious risk of destroying or damaging property by fire. Whether the phrase 'obvious risk' would be given its usual objective interpretation, as in *Elliot v C* (1983), or whether the special circumstances of this case would justify a subjective interpretation, as contemplated by their Lordships in *R v Reid* (1992), is open to question. If a subjective meaning is adopted then Jan would lack *mens rea* as she is probably unaware of the risk of damaging or destroying property by fire. However, it is more likely that the objective meaning of 'obvious risk' would be adopted in which case in seems clear that a reasonable person would foresee a

39

serious risk of damage by fire in relation to a 'very drunk' person smoking in a library. Note that the risk must be a serious one in relation to the chances of causing damage by fire, but it need not be a serious risk as far as the extent of the damage is concerned (*R v Parker* (1839)). If an 'obvious risk', in the objective sense, is established then, almost inevitably, there must have been the conscious or unconscious taking of that risk. There would be no scope for the 'lacuna' or 'loophole' argument in relation to *Caldwell* recklessness as Jan could have hardly considered the possibility of causing damage by fire and have concluded that there was no risk at all (*Chief Constable of Avon and Somerset v Shimmen* (1986)).

Jan's liability under s 1(2) and (3) of the Criminal Damage Act 1971 in relation to damaging or destroying property by fire with either an intention to endanger life, or recklessness as to whether life is endangered also requires consideration. Once again the elements of the *actus reus* are plainly satisfied in that we have been informed that property has been damaged by fire. Given the absence of intention our consideration of the *mens rea* focuses on whether Jan has consciously or unconsciously taken an obvious risk that property would be damaged by fire and that the damaged property would, in turn, endanger life (*R v Steer* (1988)). As we have already noted, in the somewhat unlikely event that a subjective meaning is given to the phrase 'obvious risk', Jan would not be liable as she almost certainly does not appreciate the risk to life. In our discussion of liability under s 1(1) and (3) above, in relation to an objective meaning of 'obvious risk', we argued that a reasonable person would foresee a serious risk of some damage by fire in the circumstances of this case. Although, it is not so clear that a reasonable person would foresee a serious risk of life being endangered as a result of property being damaged or destroyed by fire, it is quite possible that they would. In this event Jan would again be liable, notwithstanding that she is unlikely to have considered such a risk, as she would have unconsciously taken an obvious risk of life being endangered as a result of property being damaged or destroyed by fire. Once again, there seems no scope for the 'lacuna' argument for the reasons stated above.

Jan's liability for manslaughter would have to be considered in relation to the death of the two students, since she plainly lacks the intention to kill or cause grievous bodily harm necessary for murder. The *actus reus* of all forms of homicide is the same and consists of causing the death of a human-being within a year and a day (*R v Dyson* (1908)). As we have been informed that the students were killed '*in the blaze*' all the necessary elements of the *actus reus* would be present. Following the decision of the Court of Appeal in *R v Prentice and Others* (1993) it would seem that the appropriate *mens rea* for involuntary manslaughter is now that of gross negligence. A convincing argument could be put to the effect that Jan by entering the college library, almost certainly a non-smoking area, in a 'very drunk' condition has departed from the standards of reasonable behaviour. However, it is rather more arguable as to whether her conduct amounts to a sufficiently significant departure from the standards of reasonableness to constitute the gross negligence required for this form of manslaughter (*R v Bateman* (1925); *R v Prentice and Others* (1993)). Although, of course, one can not be certain, it is submitted that her conduct probably did amount to such a gross deviation from the standards of the reasonable person as to merit the application of a criminal sanction.

At the moment there seems to be some uncertainty as to whether the decision of the Court of Appeal in *R v Prentice and Others* (1993) will be interpreted in a broad sense so as to apply to all forms of involuntary manslaughter, other than constructive or motor manslaughter, or whether it will be given a narrower interpretation which limits it to cases where there is a breach of duty founded, for example, on a contractual duty. If the latter interpretation is adopted then Jan's liability in relation to reckless killing and constructive manslaughter would have to be considered.

Caldwell recklessness is the relevant form of recklessness required for reckless killing; that is the conscious or unconscious taking of an obvious and serious risk of causing death or grievous bodily harm (*R v Seymour* (1983)).

 When considering the *mens rea* concept of recklessness always specify the precise nature of the risk in question. For example, in relation to reckless killing it is the risk of death or grievous bodily harm, whereas in relation to s 1(1) of the Criminal Damage Act 1971 it is the risk of destroying or damaging property belonging to another.

Although we could not be certain, we argued above, in relation to Jan's liability for criminal damage, that a court would probably not find that Jan's case constituted the type of exceptional situation that the House of Lords in *R v Reid* (1992) indicated would justify the ascription of a subjective meaning to the phrase 'obvious risk'. Assuming, therefore, that the usual objective meaning is attached to the phrase the key issue becomes whether a reasonable person would have realised that by entering a college library whilst smoking and whilst in a very drunk condition one would create a serious risk of causing death or grievous bodily harm. Of course, we cannot be certain either way about this issue, but it does seem clear that if there is held to be an obvious risk then Jan almost certainly either consciously or unconsciously took it. This is because, just as we suggested in relation to criminal damage, there seems little scope for the 'lacuna' argument in that it is difficult to imagine how Jan could have possibly considered the risk of death or grievous bodily harm and yet have concluded that her conduct was *totally safe* (*Chief Constable of Avon and Somerset v Shimmen* (1986)).

In relation to constructive manslaughter, the three elements of the *actus reus* of a criminal, dangerous act that causes death are most probably all established on the basis of the facts provided in the scenario.

Jan's liability for s 1(1) and (3) or s 1(2) and (3) of the Criminal Damage Act 1971 would, if established, constitute the illegal and criminal action required for constructive manslaughter (*R v Arobieke* (1988)). However, in the Court of Appeal case of *R v Dalby* (1982), Waller LJ stated that where manslaughter was founded on an unlawful and dangerous act, it had to be an act directed at the victim which was likely to cause immediate injury, albeit slight. It seems clear that Jan's action was not *aimed* or directed at causing harm to the victims in this way. However, the significance of the *aimed at* doctrine has been greatly reduced, following the case of *R v Goodfellow* (1986) where it was held that *Dalby* was to be regarded primarily as an authority on causation, in that the prosecution had to establish that there had been no fresh intervening cause between the defendants act and the death of the victim. As it does appear that the students were killed as a direct and immediate result of Jan's illegal action, it would seem that the criminal act element of the *actus reus* is, indeed, established.

The unlawful act upon which constructive manslaughter is based must be a dangerous one in the sense that '... all sober and reasonable people would inevitably recognise must subject the other person to, at least the risk of some harm resulting therefrom, albeit not serious harm ...' (*per* Edmund Davies J in *R v Church* (1966)). Obviously, this is an objective test, but it leaves open the question of the precise nature of the harm which has to be reasonably foreseeable. This 'missing element' was provided by the Court of Appeal in *R v Dawson* (1985) where it was held that the possibility of some physical harm had to be reasonably foreseeable in order for the unlawful act to be a 'dangerous' one. Applying this requirement to the facts of the scenario, it seems rather unlikely that *physical harm* to the person, as distinct from damage to property, would be reasonably foreseeable in relation to a very drunk person smoking in a library.

Although the reasonable foreseeability of physical harm appears to be somewhat problematic there can be no doubt that the fire actually caused the death of the two students. If, therefore, the element of 'dangerousness' could be made out, then the *actus reus* of constructive manslaughter would be established.

In relation to the *mens rea* of constructive manslaughter, all that is required is that the defendant intends to do the act and has the fault which renders it unlawful (*DPP v Newbury and Jones* (1976)). It is irrelevant that the defendant is unaware that the act is unlawful or that it is dangerous. As we have already seen, it is at least arguable that Jan does have the necessary *mens rea* for offences contrary to either s 1(1) and (3) or s 1(2) and (3) of the Criminal Damage Act 1971. However, it would appear that Jan lacks the necessary *mens rea* for constructive manslaughter as she does not intend to do an action which is in fact both criminal and dangerous. Her only intention appears to be to smoke, an action which is obviously not criminal in itself, while the damage done to the library, although amounting to a crime, is not done intentionally.

As it seems that Jan has deliberately killed her Head of Department her liability for murder would have to be considered. The *actus reus* for all forms of homicide consists of causing the death of a human-being within a year and a day and it appears to be the case that Jan has done exactly this. However, the *mens rea* requirements seems far more problematic as Jan does not intend to kill a human-being, but the Devil. Since she is obviously suffering from a delusion her liability would depend on whether or not she could successfully found a mental defence.

Since we have been informed that Jan drank a large quantity of brandy and became very drunk it would seem that a possible defence of intoxication must be considered. If, as would appear to be the case, Jan has voluntarily become intoxicated then on the basis of the decisions of the House of Lords in *DPP v Beard* (1920), and *DPP v Majewski* (1977), she would have a defence to crimes of specific intent, but not to crimes of basic intent. The criminal damage offences, discussed above, are basic as is manslaughter, so evidence of intoxication would merely have the effect of converting these crimes into offences of strict liability as far as Jan is concerned. Murder is a crime of specific intent although it is not clear whether Jan is still intoxicated when she killed her Head of Department. In any case, as we shall see below, she will be able to rely on one of the mental defences in relation to this offence.

If Jan's intoxication was involuntary, perhaps as a result of her drinking whilst in an autonomic state caused by the shock of witnessing the injuries inflicted on Bronwen, then it would seem that she would have a defence to crimes of both specific and basic intent provided that the intoxication prevented her from forming the necessary *mens rea* or caused her to form *mens rea* that she would not have so formed were it not for the effect of the drink (*Kingston* (1993)).

In view of the fact that we have been informed that Jan was 'mad' at the time of the homicide of her Head of Department the 'mental' defences of automatism, insanity and diminished responsibility would also require consideration. The basic requirement of automatism, as Lord Denning stated in *Bratty v Attorney General for Northern Ireland* (1963), is that the defendant's muscles act without the control of her mind. Moreover, it has been established that this loss of conscious control over bodily activity must be a total, not merely a partial loss of control (*Broome v Perkins* (1987); *Attorney General's Reference (No 2) of 1992* (1993)). As we are informed that Jan became convinced that her Head of Department was the Devil it seems that she decided to kill him, a willed action that stands in sharp contrast to the autonomic behaviour that sometimes results from post traumatic stress (*R v T* (1990)). On the basis of the facts provided in the scenario, then, it seems unlikely that Jan has engaged in autonomic behaviour, what seems rather more probable is that her conduct was controlled by her mind, albeit a somewhat deluded mind. In these circumstances the relevant defence would be insanity or diminished responsibility rather than automatism.

To succeed with the defence of insanity, Jan would have to establish the existence of 'a disease of the mind' and then satisfy one or other of the rules established in *M'Naghten's* case (1843). It would seem from the facts of the scenario that Jan does, indeed, suffer from such a disease since her faculties of perception, reason, memory and understanding have been impaired in a way that clearly renders her a danger to the public (see *per* Lord Denning in *Bratty v Attorney General for Northern Ireland* (1963) and *per* Lord Diplock in *R v Sullivan* (1984)). Moreover, it does seem as if she would be able to satisfy one of the grounds for insanity laid down in the *M'Naghten* rules as the disease of the mind has caused her not to know the nature and quality of her act.

Where a defendant is found not guilty by reason of insanity the judge must make one of a number of various orders which include a hospital order with or without restrictions on discharge under s 5 of the Criminal Procedure (Insanity) Act 1964, as substituted by the Schedule 1 of the Criminal Procedure (Insanity and Unfitness to Plead) Act 1991. For this reason Jan might prefer to rely on the defence of diminished responsibility under s 2(1) of the Homicide Act 1957, which provides:

'Where a person kills or is party to a killing of another, he shall not be convicted of murder if he was suffering from such abnormality of mind (whether arising from a condition of arrested or retarded development of mind or any inherent causes or induced by disease or injury) as substantially impaired his mental responsibility for his acts and omissions in doing or being a party to the killing.'

The meaning of the phrase 'abnormality of mind' was said by Parker CJ in *R v Byrne* (1960) to be simply a state of mind that the reasonable person would find abnormal, and this was essentially a matter of fact for the jury to determine. It is, of course, extremely likely that a jury would find such an abnormality of mind in Jan's case given her strange belief about her Head of Department. This, however, is not enough on its own to establish the defence; it would also have to be established that the abnormality resulted in a substantial impairment of the defendant's self-control. The facts are too 'open' for us to be absolutely certain about this element of the defence although it seems quite possible that this was, indeed, the case. If the defence is made out the charge will be reduced from one of murder to manslaughter and, consequently, the court will not be bound to pronounce a mandatory life sentence.

Scenario 4

Austin, a hospital doctor, instructed Chantal, a nurse, to switch off a ventilating machine that had been keeping Iris, a 'brain dead' patient, alive for five months. Chantal reluctantly agreed to do this. Austin, by mistake, connected a plastic bottle containing urine to another patient's drip-feed. Julie, the patient, died after

Austin repeated the mistake on the following day. Both Iris and Julie had been the victims of a vicious knife attack by Richard. Austin had also given a lethal injection to Maureen, an elderly terminally ill patient who had been experiencing great pain and who had begged Austin to 'put me out of my misery'.

Advise, Austin, Chantal and Richard of their criminal liability. Would your advice be different if Austin had decided not to refill Julie's drip-feed instead of mistakenly connecting her to the bottle containing urine and if Iris continued to live ?

(1) Read the rubric

Quite a complicated rubric with three parties to advise and a 'sting in the tail' to cope with. Remember to underline, circle or highlight the 'sting in the tail' in order to ensure that you do not forget to deal with it after completing the discussion of the liabilities of the various parties.

(2) Read the scenario

Although this appears to be yet another complicated scenario involving several people, matters simplify somewhat when you realise that for once the facts are relatively unambiguous. Indeed, the variety of the action tends to mask the rather clear-cut nature of what has happened. Indeed, the most problematic area appears to be that of Richard's *mens rea* in relation to the attack on Julie and Iris. This becomes of crucial importance in deciding his liability for non-fatal offences in the event, suggested by the 'sting in the tail', of Iris surviving.

(3) Identify the relevant offences and defences

Austin's Liability

The only offence that Austin might possibly be liable for in the first sentence of the scenario would seem to be soliciting murder, contrary to s 4 of the Offences Against the Person Act 1861, when he instructs Chantal to switch off the ventilating machine. Similarly, there would also appear to be the possibility of a statutory conspiracy to murder, contrary to s 1(1) of the Criminal Law Act 1977, when Chantal agrees to this course of action. Of course, both these offences depend on whether what is being suggested is, indeed, a crime, but this is an issue that requires to be subjected to detailed argument rather than simply assumed one way or another.

Identify and discuss all offences that might *reasonably* have been committed by the parties in the scenario. Remember the process of constructing legal arguments is similar to doing mathematics in that the 'answer', in the sense of whether someone actually is liable or not, is not all that important. What is of crucial importance is the quality of the reasoning involved in arriving at a particular conclusion.

Austin's liability for the manslaughter of Julie will require consideration as will his liability for the murder or attempted murder of Maureen.

The only defence, as opposed to arguments concerning causation, that would appear to be available to Austin is that of necessity, although in the past the courts have rejected this plea in relation to homicide.

Chantal's liability

As we noted above, Chantal's action in disconnecting the ventilating machine raises the question of possible liability for both conspiracy to murder and murder itself. Obviously, causation will be the key issue both here and in relation to Richard's liability.

Our consideration of Chantal's liability, like that of Austin, should include a discussion of the possible defence of necessity. In addition, although 'I was just obeying orders' is not a defence in English law, the fact that a superior orders a subordinate to do something may constitute evidence of lack of *mens rea* in certain circumstances and this would require exploration.

Richard's liability

As he is responsible for the initial attacks on Iris and Julie, Richard's liability in relation to their ultimate deaths will plainly need to be considered. Clearly, issues relating to causation and *mens rea* will be of crucial importance here. In addition, Richard's liability for various non-fatal offences against the person would have to be considered in relation to the situation suggested in the 'sting in the tail' where Iris continues to live.

Figure 4 Summary of possible liability

PARTY	OFFENCE	COMMENTS	DEFENCE
Austin	Soliciting murder (s 4 OAP 1861)	No *actus reus* if no crime suggested	Necessity
	Conspiracy (s 1(1) CLA 1977)	No *actus reus* if no crime suggested	Necessity
	Manslaughter	Of Julie	Necessity
	Attempted murder (s 1(1) CAA 1981)	Of Maureen – may be alleged as an alternative to murder to avoid issues of causation	Necessity Consent
Chantal	Conspiracy (s 1(1) CLA 1977	No *actus reus* if no crime agreed upon	
	Murder	Of Iris – possibly no causation	Necessity
	Attempted murder (s 1(1) CAA 1981)	Of Iris – may be charged as an alter-native to murder to avoid issues of causation	Necessity
Richard	Murder	Of Iris and Julie	
	Manslaughter	Of Iris (if no *mens rea* for murder	
	Attempted murder (s 1(1) CAA 1981)	Of Julie (if no causation)	
	Wounding/GBH (s 18 OAP 1861)	Re Julie	
	Wounding/GBH (s 20 OAP 1861)	Re Julie (if lacking *mens rea* for s 18)	

(4)   Define the relevant offences

Having identified possible relevant offences in the manner indicated above it is then necessary to provide definitions of them. At this stage you can actually start to write your assignment or examination answer. Remember you can cite *abbreviated* statutory and common law definitions provided that all the essential elements of the offence are included. For example, murder can be simply defined as: the unlawful killing of a human-being within a year and a day with an intention to kill or cause grievous bodily harm. Obviously, such a definition begs several important questions, such as what precisely is meant by 'human-being' and 'intention', but, nevertheless, it provides us with a spring board from which we can plunge into the murky waters of legal argument.

(5)   Engage in legal reasoning

Austin's liability

Since he instructs Chantal to switch off the ventilating machine Austin may incur liability in relation to the offence of soliciting murder. By s 4 of the Offences Against the Person Act 1861, as amended by the Criminal Law Act 1977, it is an offence to '... solicit, encourage, persuade or endeavour to persuade or ... propose to any person, to murder any other person'. Although it would appear that Austin has certainly solicited Chantal to kill, it is far more problematic as to whether he has solicited her to *murder* let alone to murder a 'person'.

Whether or not Chantal has been instructed to 'murder' would depend upon whether her action is, in law, the cause of Iris's death. On the basis of the existing authorities relating to causation, this would seem extremely unlikely. In particular, the leading case of *R v Smith* (1959) established that the defendant's act would only be regarded as a cause in law if it could be shown that it was the operating and substantial cause of the victim's death. Only if the original wound could be said to have merely provided the setting in which some other cause of death operated would the courts be likely to view the chain of causation as being broken. In relation to the circumstances described in the scenario, the victim clearly died as a result of the original knife wounds; the effect of the ventilating machine being merely to suspend the fatal consequences of the initial attack (*R v Malcherek and Steel* (1981)). In short, it can be argued Austin is not instructing Chantal to 'murder' because her action would not amount, in law, to causing the death of a human-being. Only in circumstances where the decision to turn off the ventilating machine amounted to gross negligence would the causal nexus be broken and the original attacker relieved of liability (*R v Jordan* (1956)).

Alternatively, a more speculative argument could be put to the effect that Austin has not instructed Chantal to kill a *'person'*; since this term implies the existence of a conscious, thinking being. According to this line of argument, Richard attacked a *'person'* whereas Chantal has merely terminated the existence of a 'brain dead' *body* incapable of sustaining itself without mechanical assistance.

On the basis of the same arguments, Austin's liability for conspiracy to murder would appear somewhat improbable. The definition of a statutory conspiracy found in s 1(1) of the Criminal Law Act 1977 provides that it is an offence to agree:

'... that a course of conduct shall be pursued which ... either:

(a) will necessarily amount to or involve the commission of any offence ...; or

(b) would do so but for the existence of facts which render the commission of the offence impossible ...'

Of course, as we have already noted, it can be argued that Chantal does not, in law, cause the death of Iris and that, therefore, there is no agreement on a course of conduct that will *'necessarily'* involve the commission of an offence. Paragraph (b) clearly specifies that impossibility is no defence, however, the point being made here is not that the offence is impossible, but that what is being planned does not constitute an offence.

Austin's position in relation to the death of Julie would appear far less favourable. Since he does not intend to kill, the appropriate offence would be that of involuntary manslaughter. Following the Court of Appeal case of *R v Prentice and Others* (1993) it seems that there are now three categories of involuntary manslaughter: constructive manslaughter, motor manslaughter and killing by gross negligence. Clearly, killing by gross negligence would appear the appropriate offence in relation to Austin's repeated action of connecting the urine to the drip-feed. The prosecution would have to prove (1) the existence of a duty, (2) the breach of that duty and (3) gross negligence of a degree which the jury considers justifies a criminal conviction (*R v Bateman* (1925)). The first of these requirements is satisfied as a doctor obviously owes a duty of care to his patients. On the facts of the scenario it would also appear that the second requirement is satisfied. Moreover, the third and final element hardly seems anymore problematic in relation to the facts of this particular situation. In *R v Prentice and Others* the court provided a list, although not necessarily an exhaustive list, of states of mind that may properly lead a jury to make a finding of gross negligence:

'(a) Indifference to an obvious risk of injury to health.

(b) Actual foresight of the risk coupled with the determination nevertheless to run it.

(c) An appreciation of the risk coupled with an intention to avoid it but also coupled with such a high degree of negligence in the attempted avoidance as the jury considers justifies conviction.

(d) Inattention of failure to advert to a serious risk which goes beyond 'mere inadvertence' in respect of an obvious and important matter which the defendant's duty demanded he should address.'

Austin's state of mind in relation to the 'mistake' concerning the urine and the drip-feed would seem to fall within paragraph (d) above. The question for the jury, that it is submitted would, almost certainly, be answered in the affirmative is whether the failure to ascertain and use the correct drip, on two separate occasions, was '... grossly negligent to the point of criminality ...'

Unlike the position concerning the death of Iris, the grossly negligent nature of Austin's action in relation to the treatment of Julie seems to constitute a *novus actus interveniens* that would break the chain of causation and, thus, relieve, Richard, the original attacker, from liability (*R v Jordan* (1956)).

In relation to the death of Maureen, it would appear that Austin does have the requisite *mens rea* for murder in that as a doctor he surely must have foreseen the virtual certainty of death following from the administration of a 'lethal injection'. However, there would seem to be an argument that the causation element of the *actus reus* is not established in that his action resulted in only a slight acceleration of death which is, therefore, *de minimus*. There is some authority for this position, in the case of *R v Adams* (1957) Devlin J directed the jury that there is no special defence justifying a doctor in giving drugs which would shorten life in the case of severe pain: 'If life were cut short by weeks or months it was just as much murder as if it were cut short by years.' However, he went on to state:

'But that does not mean that a doctor aiding the sick or dying has to calculate in minutes or hours, or perhaps in days or weeks, the effect on a patient's life of the medicines which he administers. If the first purpose of medicine - the restoration of health - can no longer be achieved, there is still much for the doctor to do, and he is entitled to do all that is proper and necessary to relieve pain and suffering even if the measures he takes may incidentally shorten life.'

The contrast which is made in this judgment between 'weeks or months' and 'minutes and hours' does seem to support the *de minimus* argument in relation to the administration of drugs for pain saving purposes in relation to terminally patients who are already close to death. If the jury are satisfied, as they may well be on the basis of the facts provided, that Maureen was terminally ill, in severe pain and close to death then Austin would not, in law, have caused her death.

However, if Austin were charged with attempted murder then, since an attempt is by definition not a 'result' crime, there would be no need for the prosecution to establish causation and consequently no scope for the *de minimus* argument. By s 1(1) of the Criminal Attempts Act 1981 an attempt consists of intentionally doing an act '... which is more than merely preparatory to the commission of the offence ...' in question. There would seem to be no doubt that Austin has done something 'more than merely preparatory', in fact, he has done the 'last act' necessary to cause the death of Maureen. Following the Court of Appeal case of *R v Gullefer* (1990) it is clearly no longer essential to do the 'last act' necessary in order to establish the *actus reus* of attempt. However, the doctrine is still capable of providing a sound positive guide in that where the 'last act' has actually been carried out, then the defendant will certainly have done enough to have satisfied the *actus reus* requirement. Moreover, since, as we pointed out above, Austin is a doctor and has apparently administered a 'lethal injection' he would have an intention to kill and would, thus, satisfy the *mens rea* requirements of the offence. Nevertheless, as well as the defence of necessity, considered below, he could argue that the case of Adams (above) provides some authority for motive to be taken into consideration in this type of 'mercy killing'.

The defence of necessity would require consideration in relation to the offences of soliciting murder, conspiracy to murder and the murder of Maureen. In addition, the apparent consent of Maureen ought not to pass unmentioned.

At first glance it would seem that the facts described in the scenario constitute precisely the sort of situation where a defendant could be excused on the ground that he had no choice but to commit the act in question in order to avoid a greater evil. However, one of the reasons given by the House of Lords in *R v Howe* (1987) for refusing to allow a defence of duress to murder was that it had been decided in the case of *R v Dudley and Stephens* (1884) that necessity was simply not available as a defence to murder. There seems to have been two grounds for this decision, first that to allow the defence would be to contradict Christian morality which emphasised self-sacrifice and giving up one's life for others; and, secondly, that there could be no agreed criteria for selecting the victim. Arguably, Dudley and Stephens can be distinguished from the particular circumstances under consideration in that it is neither the type of situation where Austin has the option of giving up his life for another, nor one where there is a problem of selecting the victim. Therefore, as Smith and Hogan have noted, in the 7th edition of their textbook, '... notwithstanding the approval of Dudley and Stephens by Howe, it would be premature to conclude that necessity can never be a defence to murder'. Moreover, the case of *R v Martin* (1989) provides authority for the proposition that necessity, or 'duress of circumstances', as the court called it, does not necessarily have to involve a situation where the defendant's life is in danger.

Austin would be unlikely to succeed with the defence of consent in relation to the killing of Maureen. There seems little doubt that consent to being killed, to suffering grievous bodily harm and, even, to actual bodily harm is ineffective as a defence (*R v Brown and Others* (1993)).

Chantal's liability

Chantal's liability for conspiracy to murder contrary to s 1(1) of the Criminal Law Act 1977 would depend upon whether or not she has agreed on a course of conduct that would necessarily involve the commission of an offence. This, in turn, would depend upon similar arguments relating to causation as those mentioned above in relation to Austin's liability for soliciting murder.

Despite the fact that we have been informed that Chantal 'reluctantly' agreed to turn the ventilating machine off, she would, nevertheless, seem to have the requisite *mens rea* for murder. Although she probably does not desire the death of Iris she must, as a trained nurse, surely, have foreseen its virtual certainty (*R v Nedrick* (1986)). However, as we have already indicated, Chantal could argue that she did not cause the death of Iris either on grounds of *de minimus* or on the basis that, the 'brain dead', Iris was not a person at the time when the machine was switched off. If either of these arguments were to prove successful it follows that the prosecution would fail to establish causation and, therefore, the existence of an *actus reus*.

If Chantal were charged with attempted murder contrary to s 1(1) of the Criminal Attempts 1981, then, since attempt is, by definition, not a result crime, the prosecution would no longer be required to prove causation. In this situation, it is more likely that a court would hold that Chantal had brought about the *actus reus* of attempted murder by doing acts that were more than merely preparatory towards the commission of the offence in question. She could, of course, still argue that she did not intend to do acts which actually constitute an offence, but it would take a radical court to hold that 'mercy killing' did not amount to a crime.

Of course, like Austin, Chantal could raise the defence of necessity in relation to the death of Iris. The position here would be virtually identical to that discussed in relation to Austin's killing of Maureen considered above.

It is worth noting that there is no defence of 'I was just obeying orders' in English Law, so the fact that Chantal, a mere nurse, acts on the instructions of a hospital doctor would seem to be of no relevance. However, superior orders would operate to negate *mens rea*, if, for example, Austin had told Chantal to switch off the life support machine because Iris was already dead.

Richard's liability

As we have already argued, the switching off of the ventilating machine is extremely unlikely to break the chain of causation (*R v Malcherek and Steel* (1981)). Moreover, since we have been informed that Iris was kept alive for five months, it would seem that the death occurred within a period of a year and a day from the initial attack and that, consequently, the *actus reus* of homicide would be made out (*R v Dyson* (1908)). Also, because Richard carried out a 'vicious knife attack' on Iris it seems very probable that he satisfies the *mens rea* requirement of murder of an intention to kill or cause grievous bodily harm. Nevertheless, there is the somewhat remote possibility that he merely had an intention to wound, in which case he would lack the necessary mental element for murder.

If Richard did, indeed, lack the *mens rea* for murder, then, his liability for constructive manslaughter could be considered. The *actus reus* of this offence would appear to be relatively unproblematic in that the vicious knife attack on Iris would obviously amount to a dangerous criminal act which, subject to the above arguments relating to causation, resulted in death (*R v Church* (1966); *R v Arobieke* (1988)). Lord Salmon, in *DPP v Newbury and Jones* (1976), explained that in order to establish the *mens rea* for constructive manslaughter it was necessary to prove that the defendant intentionally did an act which was unlawful and dangerous, and that it was unnecessary to prove that the defendant had known that the act in question was unlawful or dangerous. Even, assuming that Richard did not intend to kill or cause grievous bodily harm when he carried out the knife attack, surely he had the requisite intention to do an act which was in fact both illegal and dangerous.

As we have already mentioned, in our discussion of Austin's liability in relation to the death of Julie, the mistaken connection of the bottle containing urine to the drip feed would probably amount to gross negligence of a sufficiently high degree to constitute an intervening act which would break the chain of causation. If this is, indeed, the case, then Richard would not have caused her death and, thus, would not have brought about the *actus reus* of any form of homicide. In these circumstances, his liability for attempted murder contrary to s 1(1) of the Criminal Attempts Act 1981 would have to be considered. The *actus reus* of this offence consists of doing an act which is more than merely preparatory to the commission of the offence of murder and by stabbing Julie it would appear that Richard has, indeed, gone beyond mere preparation. However, the position regarding the *mens rea* for this offence appears somewhat more complex.

In the case of *R v Pearman* (1985) the Court of Appeal decided that it had not been the purpose of the 1981 Act to alter the law relating to the *mens rea* of attempt. As a result decisions relating to the pre-1981 common law of attempt, such as *R v Whybrow* (1951), would still constitute binding authorities. In that case, the Court of Appeal held that it had been a misdirection for a trial judge to direct a jury on a charge of attempted murder that they should convict if the defendant had intended to kill or cause grievous bodily harm. It seems clear, therefore, that on a charge of attempted murder only an intention to kill will suffice. However, the case of *R v Walker and Hayles* (1990) indicates that this intention need not necessarily be limited to direct, purposeful, intention and that indirect or 'oblique' intention consisting of the foresight of the virtual certainty of death could also constitute the *mens rea* of attempted murder. It is, of course, not clear from the scenario whether Richard has formed either type of intention, although the fact that the knife attack is described as 'vicious' tends to indicate that maybe he did desire or foresee death as a virtual certainty. Yet again, this kind of 'open' situation calls for alternative conclusions; if Richard did have an intention to kill then he would be guilty of attempted murder, if not then his liability for various non-fatal offences would have to be considered.

There is, of course, a possibility that Richard lacked an intention to kill, but had formed an intention to cause grievous bodily harm at the time of the attack on Julie. In these circumstances his liability under s 18 of the Offences Against the Person Act 1861 for the offence of wounding or causing grievous bodily harm with intent to do grievous bodily harm comes into question. Since Richard carried out a vicious knife attack which caused sufficiently serious injuries for Julie to require hospital treatment, it seems reasonable to conclude that the *actus reus* requirements of a wound or grievous bodily harm have been satisfied. A wound requires there to have been a break in all the layers of the victim's skin and it is difficult to imagine how a 'vicious' knife attack resulting in hospitalisation could possibly result in anything less than this (*JCC v Eisenhower* (1984)). Moreover, it is not improbable that grievous bodily harm, defined by the House of Lords in *DPP v Smith* (1961) as 'really serious harm' and by the Court of Appeal in *R v Saunders* (1985) as simply 'serious harm', has also been caused.

The *mens rea* requirement for the s 18 offence is an intention to do some grievous bodily harm to the victim and, following the House of Lord's decision in *R v Hancock and Shankland* (1986)), it would appear that such an intention can be inferred by the jury from what the defendant foresaw. Richard may well have had just such an intention to cause serious harm when he launched his attack on Julie, but it is possible that he merely foresaw a wounding not amounting to grievous bodily harm, in which case he would lack the *mens rea* for the s 18 offence.

Foresight of a wound, not amounting to serious harm, is insufficient for the *mens rea* of s 18 of the Offences Against the Person Act 1861. An intention to cause serious injury is required and nothing less.

If Richard did merely intend to wound, as opposed to causing serious harm, then his liability in relation to s 20 of the Offences Against the Person Act 1861 would have to be considered. This section creates the offences of '... malicious wounding ... (or) ... maliciously inflicting grievous bodily harm ...'. As we have already pointed out, the *actus reus* requirements of a wound or grievous bodily harm are almost certainly satisfied, given that Richard committed a 'vicious' knife attack on Iris. The *mens rea* for s 20 is denoted by the word 'malicious' which the Court of Appeal in *R v Cunningham* (1957) equated with intention or recklessness, the recklessness requiring foresight on the part of the accused of harm. In the subsequent case of *R v Mowatt* (1968), Diplock LJ held that:

> 'It is quite unnecessary that the accused should have foreseen that his unlawful act might cause physical harm of the gravity described in the section, ie, a wound or serious physical injury. It is enough that he should have foreseen that some physical harm to some person, albeit of a minor character, might result.'

Richard can hardly have carried out a 'vicious' knife attack without foreseeing the risk of some physical harm to Iris and would, therefore, be 'malicious' for the purpose of the section.

Foresight of fear is insufficient for the *mens rea* of s 20 of the Offences Against the Person Act 1861. An intention to inflict some physical harm or recklessness in relation to the risk of some physical harm is required.

On the basis of the facts provided in the scenario, it would seem that, aside from the issues relating to causation and the precise nature of his *mens rea*, there are no general defences available for Richard to rely on.

The 'sting in the tail'

If Austin had decided not to refill the drip-feed then it would be necessary to reassess both his and Richard's liability in relation to the death of Julie. As far as Austin is concerned, it all depends on *why* he decided not to refill the drip-feed. If this was a reasonable medical decision taken in good faith to relieve the pain and suffering of the patient, albeit by terminating life, then, this *omission* would not constitute the gross negligence required to break the chain of causation and the attack by Richard would remain the operative and substantial cause of death. It could be argued that the fact that there was an omission to act would not be sufficient to relieve Austin of liability as he had a contractual duty to provide Julie with adequate medical care (*R v Pittwood* (1902)). The contrary argument would be that if Austin's omission to refill the drip-feed was the result of a reasonable medical decision taken in good faith with due regard to the best interests of the patient, then he would be performing rather than breaching his contractual duty.

Alternatively, if the decision by Austin was motivated by a malicious intention to seriously harm or kill Julie, then this would probably amount to an intervening cause that would relieve Richard of liability for murder, although not, of course, for the appropriate non-fatal offence.

Property Offences 4

Although the scenarios in this chapter are once again of a 'mixed' nature involving various offences, they, nevertheless tend to focus mainly on theft and related offences against property. Once again, it is a good idea to read through the concise notes in Chapter 8 concerning theft, deception and criminal damage before studying the following problem situations.

Scenario 5

Eric, an antique collecting accountancy lecturer, entered the local antique shop to make inquiries about a clock he had seen in the shop window. Inside the shop he decided to look around to see if there was anything worth stealing. He saw a Swansea teapot and decided to try to steal it. While the shopkeeper was serving another customer, Eric put the teapot in his bag. He felt guilty and replaced it before the shopkeeper returned. Eric left the shop having purchased the clock. Eric had paid the price requested by the shopkeeper which was less than on the price label because, as Eric knew, the shopkeeper had misread the price label by mistake.

Advise the parties. What difference, if any, would it make to your advice if the teapot had been kept behind the shop counter?

(1)   Read the rubric

Although you are asked to advise the parties, it will become clear on reading the scenario that it is only Eric that we need concern ourselves with. The shopkeeper is a victim rather than an offender and plainly has not incurred any criminal liability whatsoever. Remember to highlight the 'sting in the tail', it is frighteningly easy to forget to deal with this element in the heat of an examination situation.

(2)   Read the scenario

This appears to be a relatively straightforward question, if there can ever be such a thing in criminal law, which focuses on examiners' favourites such as the nature of appropriation and the operation of s 5(4) of the Theft Act 1968. Although, as we have repeatedly emphasised, you should read through the scenario without worrying too much about the law, some of these issues will inevitably occur to you at this stage. It is important that you resist the temptation to plunge in and deal with them straight away. Simply, content yourself with noting the areas of legal or factual uncertainty that will require detailed consideration at a later stage. For example, it is not clear whether Eric enters the shop with an intention to steal or whether he only forms such an intention once inside. This, as we shall see, will be of crucial importance in relation to his liability for burglary. Another area of factual uncertainty, relating to the purchase of the clock, is whether Eric selected it from the display stand and took it to the counter or whether it was selected by the shopkeeper, perhaps from behind the counter, and handed to him. Of similar significance is the uncertainty, introduced in the 'sting in the tail', as to whether Eric has entered part of a building as a trespasser by going behind the counter to get the teapot.

(3)   Identify the relevant offences and defences

Eric's liability

If Eric entered the shop with an intention to steal, and the scenario is 'open' as far as this is concerned, he would be liable for burglary contrary to s 9(1)(a) of the Theft Act 1968. Since, we are informed that once inside the shop Eric forms an intention to steal, his liability for burglary contrary to s 9(1)(b) of the Theft Act 1968 will require consideration, if only to explain why such a charge could not be sustained. As Eric 'decided to look round to see if there was anything worth stealing' the question of whether this is sufficient to found liability for attempted theft would need also to be considered. Eric's liability for theft of both the teapot and the clock would require careful consideration, not least in relation to the concept of appropriation, and the operation of s 5(4) of the 1968 Act.

A further possibility that is very easy to miss is that of Eric's liability for obtaining the clock by deception contrary to s 15 of the Theft Act 1968. Finally, a discussion of his liability in relation to the offence of making off without payment contrary to s 3 of the 1978 Theft Act.

There appears not to be any defences, other than the denial of various elements of *actus reus* or *mens rea*, that would be available to Eric in this situation.

Figure 5 Summary of possible liability

PARTY	OFFENCE	COMMENTS	DEFENCE
Eric	s 9(1)(a) TA 1968	Unlikely – no entry as a trespasser	
	s (9(1)(b) TA 1968	Unlikely – no entry as a trespasser	
	s 1(1) CAA 1981 (attempted theft of contents of shop)		
	s 1(1) TA 1968 (theft of teapot)		
	s 1(1) TA 1968 (theft of clock)	Not clear when appropriation occurs	No dishonesty
	s 15 TA 1968 (obtaining property by deception)	Is there a deception by conduct	No dishonesty
	s 3 TA 1978 (making off without payment)		
	s 9(1)(a) TA 1968	If entry as trespasser behind counter	

(4)   Define the relevant offences

Having identified the relevant offences you can begin to work your way, sentence by sentence, through the scenario discussing the liability of each party in turn. However, remember to commence your discussion of criminal liability by defining the particular offence under consideration. Some definitions are rather long-winded and consequently difficult to remember, it will help if you learn *abbreviated* definitions in these cases, but be careful not to miss out any essential elements of the offence. On other occasions you will find that virtually every word of the statutory definition will be significant. In these circumstances there is unfortunately no option but to learn the entire definition word for word. You will be able note the use of both abbreviated and full definitions, as appropriate, in the following analysis of Eric's liability.

(5)   Engage in legal reasoning

Eric's liability

As Eric has entered a shop and then proceeded to commit various offences inside, his liability for burglary contrary to s 9(1)(a) of the Theft Act 1968 should be considered. The definition of this offence can be usefully abbreviated as entering a building or part of a building as a trespasser with an intention to steal, cause grievous bodily harm, rape or do unlawful damage. The *actus reus*, therefore, consists of three elements; entry into a building (or part of a building) as a trespasser. Two of these elements are unproblematic since, obviously, there has been an entry into a building, but the issue of whether or not that entry constituted a trespass is far more problematic.

According to the civil law of trespass, which forms the basis of burglary, Eric would enter the shop as a trespasser either if he has no express or implied permission to do so, or where he exceeds that express or implied permission. Clearly, the owner of the shop will have granted permission to members of the public to enter his shop, but only for normal shopping purposes. The shopkeeper would have hardly given permission to Eric to enter *if he had known* that he had intended to steal inside. A case that illustrates this point is *R v Smith and Jones* (1976) where two friends were convicted of burglary, having stolen a television set from the house of Smith's father. The fact that they had permission to enter the house for normal domestic purposes did not prevent their entry from being a trespass when they entered with a criminal purpose in mind.

Whether or not Eric would be liable for s 9(1) burglary would, therefore, depend upon whether he entered the antique shop with a criminal purpose in mind. Whilst we cannot be certain about this it does seem from the information provided in the scenario that his entry was for normal shopping purposes; we are told that he intended to make inquiries about a clock in the window, a perfectly legitimate activity. Moreover, we are also informed that he formed an intention to look round to see if there was anything worth stealing *inside*, which tends to suggest that he had not formed this criminal intention prior to entry. If, in the rather unlikely event, that he had formed an intention to steal prior to entry, then, he would clearly be guilty of a burglary contrary to s 9(1)(a) since not only would this intention convert his entry into a trespass, but it would also satisfy one of the alternative *mens rea* conditions.

When Eric decided to look around to see if there was anything worth stealing he would, according to the same principle, transform himself from a lawful visitor into a trespasser. Moreover, as we shall see below, this looking around could be sufficient to constitute an attempted theft and so, consequently, Eric's liability for burglary contrary to s 9(1)(b) would also seem to require consideration. This version of the offence is committed where the defendant:

'having entered any building or part of a building as a trespasser ... steals or attempts to steal anything in the building ... or inflicts or attempts to inflict ... any grievous bodily harm'.

Although Eric is certainly a trespasser from the moment he forms the intention to steal, and may have done enough to amount to an attempt, he will only be liable under s 9(1)(b) if he has *entered* as a trespasser and this, as we noted above, appears somewhat improbable on the basis of the facts provided. However, useful marks can sometimes be gained by explaining precisely why a defendant will not be liable in circumstances that tend to suggest a particular offence.

 Useful marks can sometimes be gained by explaining precisely why a defendant would not be liable in circumstances where the fact situation tends to suggest a particular offence.

The position so far, regarding liability for both types of burglary, can be summarised as follows: provided Eric had already formed an intention to steal prior to entering the shop, then he would commit a s 9(1)(a) burglary when he steps over the threshold and a s 9(1)(b) when he steals or attempts to steal inside. If, however, he has not formed an intention to steal prior to entry, then he would not be liable for either s 9(1)(a) or s 9(1)(b) as he would not have entered as a trespasser.

As we have already mentioned, when Eric looks round to see if there is anything worth stealing, he may incur liability for attempted theft. An attempt contrary to s 1(1) of the Criminal Attempts Act 1981 can be defined as intentionally '... doing an act which is more than merely preparatory to the commission of the offence ...' in question. The fact that Eric does not appear to have an intention to steal a specific object, but a conditional intention to steal something of worth, will not relieve him of liability as he can be charged with attempting to steal some or all of the contents of the shop (*Attorney General's References (Nos. 1 and 2 of 1979)* (1980)). Moreover, as impossibility is no defence to a charge of attempt, Eric cannot successfully argue that there was nothing worth stealing in the shop (*R v Shivpuri* (1985)).

However, the issue of whether Eric had done something more than merely preparatory to stealing by simply looking around the shop would appear to be somewhat more problematic. Prior to the Act the old common law of sufficient proximity was expressed in various ways which required that only 'the last act' or an act 'immediately connected' with the offence could be an attempt (*R v Eagleton* (1855); *DPP v Stonehouse* (1978)). Indeed, some of the early decisions following the enactment of the Criminal Attempts Act 1981 appeared to assume that this very restrictive common law approach still represented the law (*R v Widdowson* (1986)). Nevertheless, in *R v Gullefer* (1990), Lord Lane disapproved of this approach and said that the Act sought 'to steer a midway course' between mere preparation on the one hand and the last act necessary to commit the offence on the other.

Of course, whether an act is 'more than merely preparatory to the commission of an offence' is a question of fact. The judge will decide whether there is sufficient evidence to support such a finding and then the jury will decide (1) what acts the defendant did and (2) whether they were more than merely preparatory. It may well be that a jury would find that when Eric looked round the local antique shop with an intention to steal, particularly if the shop was small with many items on open display and within easy reach, he had ventured beyond Lord Lane's midway point.

 Always relate each element of the *actus reus* and *mens rea* to the particular facts under consideration.

Eric may well become liable for theft when he places the teapot in his bag. Section 1(1) of the Theft Act 1968 provides that a person is guilty of theft if he:

'... dishonestly appropriates property belonging to another with the intention of permanently depriving the other of it...'.

The three elements of the *actus reus*, appropriation, property and the concept of belonging to another all appear to be satisfied. Appropriation constitutes the central conduct of theft and is defined in s 3(1):

'Any assumption by a person of the rights of an owner amounts to an appropriation, and this includes, where he has come by the property (innocently or not) without stealing it, any later assumption of a right to it by keeping or dealing with it as owner.'

In placing the teapot in his bag, Eric would clearly be assuming one of the rights of an owner, that of physically controlling the property. Moreover, in *R v MacPherson* (1973) the court had little hesitation in finding that similar behaviour could amount to an appropriation, a view further endorsed by Lord Roskill in his speech in the House of Lords case of *R v Morris* (1984).

Equally clearly, the teapot would constitute property for the purposes of theft according to the definition provided in s 4(1) where it is stated that:

'"Property" includes money and all other property, real or personal, including things in action and other intangible property.'

Although this seemingly wide definition is limited in certain respects by subsequent subsections, a tangible object such as a teapot would undoubtedly fall within it's ambit.

Similarly, there is little doubt that the teapot does 'belong to another' within the meaning of s 5(1) which provides that:

'Property shall be regarded as belonging to any person having possession or control of it, or having in it any proprietary right or interest (not being an equitable interest arising only from an agreement to transfer or grant an interest).'

Clearly the section does not require that property should be owned by the person from whom it is appropriated, mere possession or even control is sufficient. So even if the shopkeeper does not own the teapot, perhaps because he has stolen it himself, it would still amount to property belonging to another as against Eric for the purposes of the law of theft.

The establishment of *mens rea* in relation to the theft of the teapot would appear to be just as unproblematic as the *actus reus* requirements considered above. It appears that Eric would not come within any of the negative concepts of dishonesty contained within s 2, ie, honest belief in a legal right to the property, honest belief in the other's consent, or honest belief that the owner cannot be discovered by taking reasonable steps. Indeed, his feeling of guilt immediately subsequent to the appropriation of the teapot, can hardly be reconciled with any of the honest beliefs required for s 2.

It is clear, however, that a defendant, like Eric, who does not fall within the negative definition of dishonesty contained in s 2(1) may, nevertheless, escape liability if the jury does not consider his actions to be blameworthy. In short, s 2(1) provides a negative test of dishonesty, but not a positive one. Following *R v Feely* (1973), it is no longer permissible for a trial judge to withdraw the issue of dishonesty from the jury by directing them that, as a matter of law, the defendant's actions were dishonest. The matter should now be left to the jury to decide in accordance with their own standards of decent behaviour. In this respect the Court of Appeal's decision in *R v Ghosh* (1982) has come to represent something of a 'model direction' for theft cases. The court held that in cases of doubt, where the defendant did not come within the s 2(1) negative definition, the jury should be asked:

'Was the defendant dishonest according to the standards of ordinary decent people? If yes, did the defendant realise that what he was doing was dishonest by these standards?'

There seems little doubt that 'ordinary decent people' would, indeed, consider the placing of the teapot in the bag as dishonest, particularly as the action was accompanied by an intention to steal. Moreover, the fact that Eric felt 'guilty' about it is evidence that he must surely have realised that his behaviour would be regarded in this way.

Although, as we have argued, Eric certainly appears to be dishonest, there remains the issue of whether or not he had an 'intention to permanently deprive'. Once again, this seems relatively straightforward, notwithstanding the fact that he replaced the teapot almost immediately. It is his intention at the time he appropriated the teapot by putting it in his bag that matters, and surely he did have an intention to permanently deprive at that precise moment. Indeed, in view of the fact that he 'decided to try to steal' the teapot, it is difficult to imagine any other reason for placing it in his bag other than an intention to permanently deprive. Moreover, his subsequent feelings of guilt may well have been generated in response to this earlier intention to permanently deprive the rightful owner of his property.

We are informed that Eric purchased 'the' clock, ie, the clock he originally saw in the shop window, but it is not clear whether he or the shopkeeper picked it up and returned it to the counter. Obviously, if the shopkeeper retrieved the clock there would be no question of a theft by Eric occurring at this stage. If, however, it was Eric who went and collected the clock from the window then the position is not so clear. In these circumstances a consideration of whether a theft could have possibly occurred at the moment of selection from the window display would be required, if only to ultimately dismiss this possibility. Remember your lecturer or examiner will be more interested in the quality of your legal reasoning than in the actual conclusions you eventually arrive at. Obviously, the clock both falls within the s 4(1) definition of property and the s 5(1) definition of property belonging to another. What is not so clear is whether or not there is an appropriation in these circumstances.

An initial point worth making is that since the clock was apparently correctly priced, the issues raised by this case are distinct from those in *Dip Kaur v Chief Constable of Hampshire* (1981) where the customer selected goods that were mistakenly underpriced by the retailer. Here we are concerned with the question of whether the honest shopper who selects goods from a display appropriates the items so selected. Two alternative arguments can be put in relation to this situation. The prosecution case would be that since handling the property is one of the rights of the owner and that, according to the House of Lords decision in *R v Gomez* (1992), consent is irrelevant, there is an appropriation in these circumstances. An opposing argument would be that in order for the concept of appropriation to retain any meaning at all there must be, as Lord Roskill stated in *Morris*, an *adverse* interference with the rights of the owner. This requirement could be reconciled with *Gomez* on the grounds that it is only when consent is produced by some form of deception that it becomes irrelevant to appropriation.

However, both the above arguments are somewhat academic since Eric would plainly lack the dishonesty element of the *mens rea* required for theft when he selects the clock from the window display. It would seem that he would fall within the negative definition of dishonesty contained in s 2(1)(b) as he probably has an honest belief that he would have the shopkeeper's consent to pick up the clock and return it to the counter. Even if this argument fails, it seems extremely unlikely, applying the *Ghosh* direction, that ordinary decent people would regard his actions as dishonest, let alone Eric himself realise that they would be so regarded. In addition, it can be argued that he has no intention to permanently deprive at this point since he intends handing the clock over to the shopkeeper at the counter.

There is, of course, another possibility of Eric incurring liability for theft at the counter when he purchases the clock for what he knows to be the wrong price. In relation to the *actus reus* of theft, only the fact that the clock constitutes property within the meaning of s 4(1) remains unproblematic.

Clearly, the same sort of considerations relating to appropriation as those above would also apply in this situation. Although the prosecution argument would be considerably strengthened by the allegation that Eric did, on this occasion, obtain the consent of the owner to take the clock by deception. The deception in question would consist of Eric's conduct in representing that he honestly believed the price requested by the shopkeeper to be correct when he knew that this was not the case (*DPP v Ray* (1974)). However, the problem with this argument is that the deception was not operative in that the price was determined by the shopkeeper prior to Eric's conduct. Whether or not there is an appropriation in these circumstances hinges, then, on whether consent is simply irrelevant or whether it requires an operative deception to render it so. Unfortunately, there are *dicta* in *Gomez* that seem to support both positions, although on grounds of logic the latter interpretation is clearly preferable.

In addition to the complex considerations relating to the concept of appropriation there is also the issue of whether the clock belongs to another. Having purchased the clock, albeit at the wrong price, Eric could argue that it became his, and that a charge of theft could not be sustained because it was no longer property belonging to another. The counter argument would be that this situation falls within the ambit of s 5(4) of the 1968 Act which provides that:

'Where a person gets property by another's mistake, and is under an obligation to make restoration ... of the property or its proceeds ... then to the extent of that obligation the property or its proceeds shall be regarded (as against him) as belonging to the person entitled to restoration ...'

At first glance, this section would appear to prevent the property in the clock from passing to Eric, because of the shopkeeper's mistake concerning the price. The main problem, from the prosecution point of view, is that s 5(4) does not of itself create an obligation to restore goods obtained as a result of another's mistake. Such an obligation must be a legal one, under the existing civil law, not merely a moral one (*R v Gilks* (1972)). It has been clearly established that such an obligation does exist where money is obtained as a result of another's mistake (*Attorney General's Reference (No 1 of 1983)* (1984)), but the position is uncertain as regards other forms of property. On civil law principles it would seem that an obligation to make restoration cannot arise, at least in the case of a voidable contract, until it is actually avoided, usually by informing the defendant of this fact.

However, in the criminal cases, such as *Lawrence* (1972) and *R v Gomez* (1992), where consent has been held to be irrelevant in relation to appropriation there has been a tendency to treat the question of whether the property belongs to another as unproblematic as well. In this way the complex issues of civil law relating to s 5(4) could be successfully avoided by the prosecution.

Even if the '*Lawrence*'/'*Gomez*' view of appropriation is accepted and the property held to belong to another, with or without the invocation of s 5(4), there remains the issue of whether Eric has been dishonest. Just as we noted in relation to the 'theft' of the clock from the window, Eric could argue that he would fall within the statutory negative definition of dishonesty, on this occasion the relevant section being s 2(1)(a). Under this subsection a person will not be dishonest if he honestly believes that he has a legal right to the property, and it may well be that Eric has just such a belief, indeed, in terms of contract law he would have acquired a voidable title to the clock. Even if Eric does not come within of s 2(1) he would still be able to argue that, under the *Ghosh* test, 'ordinary decent people' would operate a sort of 'let the seller beware' principle and, therefore, not consider his behaviour to have been dishonest. In the event of this argument being rejected, Eric would still have a defence under the subjective limb of the *Ghosh* test in that he could claim that he did not realise that his conduct would be regarded as dishonest by ordinary decent people. Whether or not this latter argument succeeds would depend, perhaps, upon the amount by which the price of the clock was mis-stated by the shopkeeper.

Although, as we have seen, the question of dishonesty appears to be somewhat problematic, clearly there does seem to be an intention to permanently deprive the owner of the clock.

In addition to theft, Eric's liability for obtaining the clock by deception should also be considered. The offence of obtaining property by deception is created by s 15(1) of the Theft Act 1968 which provides:

'A person who by any deception dishonestly obtains property belonging to another, with the intention of permanently depriving the other of it, shall on conviction on indictment be liable to imprisonment for a term not exceeding ten years.'

Most of the elements of the *actus reus* appear to be present in that Eric 'obtains property belonging to another'. However, the position is rather more complex concerning whether or not there has been a deception on his part. As we have already noted, in our consideration of theft, the prosecution could argue that there was a deception based on conduct, but there would be difficulties in establishing that this was an operative deception. Surely, the shopkeeper asked for the wrong amount *before* there could have been any deception and for a deception to be operative it must precede the obtaining of property (*R v Collis-Smith* (1971)).

In the somewhat unlikely event that the above argument failed, and it was held that Eric's conduct did amount to the *actus reus* of obtaining property by deception, there would still be problems for the prosecution in establishing the necessary *mens rea* for the offence. Unlike dishonesty in theft, to which s 2(1) applies, there is no negative definition of dishonesty applicable to deception offences. However, the judge should read out the *Ghosh* direction to the jury in cases where dishonesty is in issue. As we noted, above, Eric would be able to present an argument to the effect that he was not dishonest under both the objective and subjective limbs of the *Ghosh* test. If Eric is found to be dishonest, then the prosecution will have few problems establishing the remaining element of the *mens rea* in that he clearly had an 'intention of permanently depriving' the shopkeeper of the clock.

Eric's liability for the offence of making off without payment should also be considered. Section 3(1) of the Theft Act 1978 provides:

'... a person who, knowing that payment on the spot for any goods supplied or services done is required or expected from him, dishonestly makes off without having paid as required or expected and with intent to avoid payment of the amount due shall be guilty of an offence.'

Two of the three elements of the *actus reus* would appear to be satisfied in that the clock constitutes 'goods' and that Eric has 'made off' in the sense of having left the spot where payment is due (*R v McDavitt* (1981)). However, it is rather more problematic as to whether he has made off 'without having paid as required or expected'. Failing to make any payment at all would clearly satisfy this requirement, as would leaving an inadequate amount, but it seems that Eric has paid as required and expected by the shopkeeper.

In the event of the above argument relating to the *actus reus* of the offence being rejected, Eric could still claim that he was not objectively or subjectively dishonest according to the *Ghosh* test. The arguments here are essentially the same as those we have already noted in relation to theft.

The 'sting in the tail'

If the teapot had been kept behind the shop counter then Eric's liability for burglary contrary to s 9(1)(a) of the Theft Act 1968 would have to be reassessed. Clearly, the space behind the counter constitutes 'part of a building' which customers would not have permission to enter (*R v Walkington* (1979)). Therefore, the only issue relating to the *actus reus* of burglary, that is entering a building or part of a building as a trespasser, is whether Eric has effected an *entry*. On the basis of the Court of Appeal decision in *R v Collins* (1973) an entry must be 'substantial and effective'. What constitutes such an entry will depend on the circumstances, but in *R v Brown* (1985), it was held that leaning into a broken shop window to extract goods would be sufficient. In view of these two decisions it seems reasonable to conclude that Eric did enter part of the building as a trespasser since he must have either reached over the counter or walked round behind it in order to pick up the teapot. One of the alternative *mens rea* requirements for s 9(1)(a) burglary is evident here as, at the moment he places the teapot in his bag, Eric surely has an intention to steal it.

Scenario 6

Clare was a pickpocket. She entered 'Tramps' night-club to wait for a suitable victim to ask her to dance. Eventually, she was asked to dance by, Andrew, a young lecturer with a bulging wallet. During Andrew's wilder gyrations, Clare managed to remove his wallet without him noticing and hid it down the front of her dress. Shortly afterwards Andrew discovered that his wallet was missing when he uncharacteristically tried to pay for a drink. He immediately suspected Clare of the theft and began to shake her and cry for help. The wallet dropped out from under Clare's dress and in the confusion she ran out of the night-club pushing a customer out of the way. Outside, Clare stopped a passing motorist, telling him that she urgently needed to visit her child who was seriously ill in hospital. The motorist drove Clare to the hospital.

Discuss the criminal liability of the parties.

(1)   Read the rubric

A deceptively straightforward rubric that might lead the unwary student to concentrate exclusively on Clare's liability. Although, a discussion of Clare's liability is obviously central to this scenario, the position of both Andrew and the motorist should also be considered.

(2)   Read the scenario

A relatively unproblematic situation. The only factual uncertainties seem to relate to the severity of the 'shaking' inflicted on Clare and the extent of the injuries, if any, suffered by the customer.

(3)   Define the relevant offences and defences

Clare's liability

When Clare enters the night-club with an intention to steal therein she may commit an offence contrary to s 9(1)(a) of the Theft Act 1968. Once inside, the question of whether she has done enough to amount to attempted theft by simply waiting for someone to ask her to dance would also require consideration, if only to conclude that she has not. Later, when she removes Andrew's wallet, her liability for both theft and a second burglary, this time contrary to s 9(1)(b) of the Theft Act 1968, should be considered.

Clare's action of pushing the customer out of the way will necessitate a consideration of her liability for a range of non-fatal offences against the person since the facts are 'open' as to the extent of the injuries suffered. These would include common assault and battery, an assault occasioning actual bodily harm and malicious wounding or inflicting grievous bodily harm contrary to s 47 and s 20 of the Offences Against the Person Act 1861 respectively.

If, as seems likely, Clare told the passing motorist a lie in order to persuade him to give her a lift, her liability in relation to the offence of obtaining services by deception contrary to s 1(1) of the Theft Act 1978 should be discussed.

There do not seem to be any relevant defences, as distinct from alleging that certain elements of the *actus reus* and *mens rea* have not been made out, that Clare would be able to raise.

Andrew's liability

The only possible criminal liability in relation to Andrew occurs when he shakes Clare. The issue of whether this action could amount to a common assault and battery or possibly an assault occasioning actual bodily harm, contrary to s 47 of the Offences Against the Person Act 1861, ought to be discussed.

In particular, your consideration of Andrew's liability should focus on the common law defence of self-defence and the statutory defence under s 3(1) of the Criminal Law Act 1967.

The liability of the motorist

Very briefly the liability of the motorist for impeding the apprehension or prosecution of an offender contrary to s 4 of the Criminal Law Act 1967 should be considered.

Figure 6   Summary of possible liability

PARTY	OFFENCE	COMMENTS	DEFENCE
Clare	s 9(1)(a) TA 1968 (burglary)	Committed on entry to nightclub	
	s 1(1) CAA 1981 (attempted theft)	Unlikely to have gone beyond mere preparation	
	s 1(1) TA 1968 (theft)	Theft of wallet	
	s 9(1)(b) TA 1968 (burglary)	Occurs with theft of the wallet	
	Assault and battery	If no hurt or injury suffered	
	s 47 OAP 1861	If minor injury	
	s 20 OAP 1861	If wound or serious injury	
	s 8(1) TA 1968 (robbery)	Violence not used in order to steal	
	s 1(1) TA 1978 (obtaining services by deception)	Obtains lift by deception	
Andrew	Assault and battery	By shaking Clare	Self-defence (s 3(1) CLA 1967)
	s 47 OAP 1861	If minor injury	Self-defence (s 3(1) CLA 1967)
Motorist	s 4 CLA 1967	*Mens rea* unlikely	

(5)   Define the relevant offences

Remember to commence the process of legal reasoning by providing, as appropriate, a full or abbreviated definition of the offence in question. Indeed, many apparently puzzling issues can often be resolved, or at least simplified, merely by referring to an accurately stated definition. Of course, by this stage we have become familiar with this process having already stated, in some cases more than once, the definitions of most of the main offences encountered on a typical course in criminal law. However, different constituent elements of these definitions will themselves frequently require further clarification by reference to case law, statutory provisions or principled argument, depending upon the specific facts of the scenario under consideration. The various scenarios have been designed to show you how this process of definition and sub-definition can vary according to which elements are problematic in relation to the facts under consideration.

(6)   Engage in legal reasoning

Clare's liability

When Clare enters the night-club she may be committing a burglary. Section 9(1)(a) of the Theft Act 1968, provides that a person is guilty of burglary if '... he enters a building or part of a building as a trespasser ... with intent to ...' steal, or inflict grievous bodily harm, or rape, or do any unlawful damage therein. As far as the *actus reus* is concerned, since Clare has plainly entered a building, the only problematic issue would appear to be whether she entered as a trespasser.

The civil law concept of trespass forms the basis of burglary; if there is no civil trespass there can be no burglary. In essence a civil trespass simply consists of entering a building either without express permission or in circumstances where the defendant exceeds the express or implied permission. Although members of the public would have permission to enter 'Tramps' and would not, therefore, be trespassers, that permission, no doubt, would be conditional on the entry being for the purposes of normal night-club activities. The owners of the club would have hardly granted permission to enter to Clare if they had known that she intended to steal from their customers (*R v Smith and Jones* (1976)). However, while it is essential that the defendant is a trespasser in terms of the civil law, this alone is not enough. Liability for the tort of trespass is strict in that a mistake, even a reasonable one, is no defence to a civil action. Nevertheless, in order to commit burglary a mental element is required in relation to the trespass element of the *actus reus* in that the defendant must know or, at least, be reckless as to the facts which render the entry a trespass (*R v Collins* (1973)).

Although Clare may have realised that she would not have permission to enter the night-club had the owners known of her criminal purpose, there remains the possibility that she gave no thought at all to this eventuality. Despite the lack of direct authority on the point, the academic textbook writers seem to be all of the opinion that the recklessness envisaged here is 'subjective' as in *R v Cunningham* (1957) and not 'objective' as in *MPC v Caldwell* (1982). If this is, indeed, the case then failure to consider even the risk of an entry without express or implied permission would be insufficient to establish a trespass for the purposes of the criminal law.

However, assuming that the *actus reus* of burglary has been established, the *mens rea* would appear to be relatively unproblematic in that Clare clearly entered the building with an intention to steal therein.

The issue of whether Clare has done enough to amount to an attempted theft by simply waiting for a victim to ask her to dance should also be considered.

Section 1(1) of the Criminal Attempts Act 1981 provides that an attempt occurs:

'If, with intent to commit an offence ... a person does an act which is more than merely preparatory to the commission of the offence ...'.

According to Lord Lane CJ, in *R v Gullefer* (1990), the *actus reus* of the offence occurs 'when the merely preparatory acts come to an end and the defendant embarks upon the crime proper'. It is submitted that by waiting to be asked to dance, Clare is unlikely to have 'embarked upon the crime proper'. Of course, it might be otherwise if she had been waiting for an opportunity to pick the pocket of anyone standing next to her; in these circumstances she, surely, could be said to be about the business of pickpocketing. If, in the somewhat unlikely event of the *actus reus* of attempt being made out, then the establishment of the *mens rea* would appear to be unproblematic in that she has plainly formed an intention to steal.

When Clare actually removes Andrew's wallet she would undoubtedly commit the offence of theft contrary to s 1(1) of the Theft Act 1968 which provides:

'A person is guilty of theft if he dishonestly appropriates property belonging to another with the intention of permanently depriving the other of it ...'

Both the *actus reus* and the *mens rea* appear to be unproblematic. Obviously, the wallet and its contents constitute 'property' within the meaning of s 4(1), and clearly they 'belong to another' within the meaning of s 5(1). Even the normally complex issue of appropriation is straightforward in this case as the removal of Andrew's wallet would clearly constitute an assumption of the rights of an owner in accordance with s 3(1).

On the *mens rea* side not only do none of the negative definitions of dishonesty contained in s 2(1) apply, but also it is difficult to see how positive dishonesty could become an issue. Nevertheless, following *R v Feely* (1973) it is no longer permissible for a trial judge to withdraw the issue of dishonesty from a jury by directing them that, as a matter of law, the defendant's actions were dishonest. In cases where the defendant cannot avail herself of s 2(1), and where there is some dispute as to whether or not her actions were dishonest, the matter should be left to the jury to determine. The Court of Appeal, in *R v Ghosh* (1982), held that in cases of doubt the jury should be directed as follows:

'Was the defendant dishonest according to the standards of ordinary decent people? If yes, did the defendant realise that what he was doing was dishonest by these standards?'

It is, of course, virtually impossible to imagine that Clare's conduct would not be considered as dishonest under both the objective and the subjective limbs of the *Ghosh* test. Similarly, Clare would appear to satisfy the other requirement of the *mens rea* of theft of an intention to permanently deprive the owner of the property. The fact that she eventually drops the wallet and leaves it behind is irrelevant as it is her intention at the moment of appropriation that matters.

Avoid being distracted by 'red-herrings' in the scenario. For example, in theft scenarios, the 'stolen property' is sometimes returned or left behind very shortly after the appropriation. There are two points to remember about this. Firstly there is no need for the owner to actually be permanently deprived of the property, all that is required is an *intention to permanently deprive* on the part of the defendant. Secondly, it is the moment of appropriation which is the relevant moment for this intention; the fact that the defendant subsequently forms an intention to return the property is of no relevance.

By committing the theft of the wallet, Clare would automatically, given that she entered the night-club as a trespasser, also become liable for a further offence of burglary. Section 9(1)(b) of the Theft Act 1968, which creates this second form of burglary, provides:

> 'A person is guilty of burglary if having entered any building or part of a building as a trespasser he steals or attempts to steal anything in the building or that part of it or inflicts or attempts to inflict on any person therein any grievous bodily harm.'

As we have already noted, Clare may well have originally entered the building as a trespasser and has, almost certainly, committed a theft inside. In these circumstances she would also satisfy the requirements for a burglary contrary to s 9(1)(b).

Clare's liability for various non-fatal offences against the person would have to be considered in relation to her action in pushing the customer out of the way. At the very least she would be liable for a common battery and most probably a common assault as well. Assault and battery were two distinct crimes at common law, but following the enactment of s 39 of the Criminal Justice Act 1988, are likely to be charged as two separate statutory offences (*DPP v Little* (1991)). An assault is any act by which the defendant, intentionally or recklessly, causes the victim to apprehend immediate and unlawful personal violence (*Fagan v MPC* (1969)). A battery is any act by which the defendant, intentionally or recklessly, inflicts unlawful personal violence upon a victim (*R v Rolfe* (1952)). The authorities seem quite clear that 'violence' here includes any unlawful touching of another, however slight (*R v Thomas* (1985)).

Since we are informed that Clare has pushed a customer out of the way there would appear to be little doubt as far as the *actus reus* of a battery is concerned. Moreover, as the word 'pushed' tends to indicate a purposeful action it would seem that the *mens rea* requirement of an intention to inflict unlawful violence is also satisfied. Whether or not an assault has occurred is somewhat more problematic. In relation to the *actus reus* the facts are 'open' as to whether or not the customer actually apprehended immediate unlawful violence. However, given that he would have been alerted by Andrew's cry for help he may well have been aware of Clare's proximity and possibly feared unlawful violence.

As far as the *mens rea* is concerned, it seems unlikely that Clare intended to cause the customer to fear unlawful violence, so her liability will depend on whether or not she was reckless in this respect. Following some uncertainty on the point, the House of Lords decision in *R v Savage* (1991) seems to have clarified the position by assuming that is the *Cunningham* not *Caldwell* type of recklessness which is required. It follows that if Clare foresaw the risk of causing apprehension of violence as a consequence of effecting her rapid departure from the night-club, she would have the necessary *mens rea* for an assault.

The facts of the scenario are 'open' as to whether the customer suffered any injuries as a result of being pushed out of the way by Clare. If slight injuries were in fact caused then Clare's liability for an assault occasioning actual bodily harm would need to be considered. The *actus reus* of this offence, contained in s 47 of the Offences Against the Persons Act 1861, requires proof of three elements, an assault, causation and actual bodily harm. The word 'assault' is used in this section to mean either an assault or a battery, and, as we have already noted, Clare has, almost certainly, committed a battery and, quite possibly, an assault as well. If we assume that Clare's action of pushing the customer resulted in injury then the causation element would obviously be satisfied. The final element of the *actus reus*, the actual bodily harm has been defined as any hurt or injury likely to interfere with the health or comfort of the victim (*R v Miller* (1954)). Such a broad definition would seem to cover even relatively minor injuries such as bruising, sprained joints, grazing and concussion. It seems, then, that if the battery inflicted by Clare caused any injury at all, the *actus reus* of the s 47 offence would be made out.

Although s 47 does not expressly stipulate any *mens rea* requirement the courts have interpreted it to imply either intention or recklessness (*R v Venna* (1976)). Not only has it been decided that the recklessness in question is of the subjective *Cunningham* type, but also that the *mens rea* need not extend beyond the initial assault to the consequent actual bodily harm (*R v Savage* (1991)). This means that as long as Clare either intended or was reckless in relation to the unlawful touching of the customer, then she would satisfy the *mens rea* requirements of s 47, this would be so even if she had not foreseen any resulting physical harm at all. It would appear, then, provided an injury has resulted from her action, that Clare could well be liable for the s 47 offence.

If the customer suffered a wound or serious bodily harm as a result of being pushed out of the way, then Clare's liability for a more serious offence would have to be considered. Section 20 of the Offences Against the Person Act 1861 creates what are, in effect, two separate offences of '... malicious wounding ...' and '... maliciously inflicting grievous bodily harm ...'. In order to constitute a wound all the layers of the victim's skin must have been broken, therefore, if the customer suffers merely a graze, or even internal bleeding, this will not suffice to establish a wound (*JCC v Eisenhower* (1984)). Alternatively the *actus reus* would be established if the customer sustained 'serious harm' such as a fractured limb, or the rupturing of internal organs (*R v Saunders* (1985)).

The *mens rea* of being 'malicious', stipulated in the definition of the offence, has been interpreted to mean either intention or recklessness in the subjective *Cunningham* sense of the conscious taking of an unjustified risk of some physical harm (*R v Mowatt* (1968)). It follows that if Clare foresaw the risk of some physical harm, however slight, resulting from her action of pushing the customer out of the way, she would have the necessary mental element for the s 20 offence.

Since Clare appears to have both stolen and used force her liability in relation the offence of robbery should be briefly considered. Section 8(1) of the Theft Act 1968 provides that:

'A person is guilty of robbery if he steals, and immediately before or at the time of doing so, and in order to do so, he uses force on any person or puts or seeks to put any person in fear of being then and there subjected to force.'

Clearly, Clare would not be liable for this offence because she did not use force immediately before or at the time of the theft. Moreover, it is plain that she does not use force in order to steal, but in order to escape.

When Clare stops a passing motorist and tells him what is presumably a lie to persuade him to give her a lift, she may have committed the offence of obtaining services by deception. Section 1(1) of the Theft Act 1978 simply states that:

'A person who by any deception dishonestly obtains services from another shall be guilty of an offence.'

The Act provides a partial definition of 'services' in s 1(2) which states:

'It is an obtaining of services where the other is induced to confer a benefit by doing some act, or causing or permitting some act to be done, on the understanding that the benefit has been or will be paid for.'

Whether or not a service is beneficial appears to be a subjective matter in each case and there seems little doubt that the lift to the hospital would be of benefit to Clare in that it removes her from the scene of the crime. Moreover, there appears to be an operative deception by words in that the motorist has been induced by Clare's lie to provide the service in the belief that he is carrying out a humanitarian action. However, the words '... on the understanding that the benefit has been or will be paid for ...', in s 1(2), have the effect of excluding gratuitous services from the scope of the offence. It is this element which does not on the facts appear to be satisfied as the motorist is under no illusion that he will be paid for the journey.

If, despite the above argument, the *actus reus* of the offence is made out then the *mens rea* question of dishonesty will be left to the jury to consider on the basis of the *Ghosh* direction.

Andrew's liability

Andrew's action in shaking Clare raises the issue of his liability for assault and battery. It appears that the *actus reus* and *mens rea* requirements of these two separate offences, which we have already discussed in relation to Clare's liability, would be satisfied in the circumstances under consideration. The main issue would be whether or not Andrew could put up a valid defence. It seems quite clear that the common law of self-defence includes the use of reasonable force in order to defend property (*Attorney General's Reference No 2 of 1983* (1984)). However, it could be argued that Andrew was using force to apprehend a suspect rather than to protect his property; since at the time he began to shake Clare he did not know for certain that she was in possession of his wallet.

In addition to the common law defence of self-defence, there is a statutory defence contained in s 3(1) of the Criminal Law Act 1967 which provides that:

'A person may use such force as is reasonable in the circumstances in the prevention of crime, or in effecting or assisting in the lawful arrest of offenders or suspected offenders or of persons unlawfully at large.'

Whilst Andrew would not be using force in the prevention of crime as the theft had already occurred, it does seem as if he was trying to effect the arrest of a suspected offender. In these circumstances all that would remain to be established would be whether the force used was reasonable or not. Clearly by shaking Clare, Andrew has used a degree of force that was more than strictly necessary to effect an arrest; simply holding her would have sufficed. The central issue, therefore, would be whether the apparently excessive use of force was sufficient to negate the defence. In *Palmer v R* (1971), Lord Morris held that the test to be applied was an objective one, ie, whether a reasonable person would have acted as the defendant had in the same circumstances, but, nevertheless, recognised that '... a person defending himself cannot weigh to a nicety the exact measure of his necessary defensive action'. Consequently, it is, perhaps, doubtful whether a jury would find the degree of force used to be excessive in the circumstances of the scenario.

The liability of the motorist

The only offence that the motorist could possibly have committed it that of impeding the apprehension or prosecution of offenders contrary to s 4(1) of the Criminal Law Act 1967. However, because it seems clear that he did not know or believe Clare to have committed an offence and since, consequently, he did not intend to impede her apprehension, he would lack the necessary *mens rea*.

Scenario 7

Nick was making alterations to his flat and was in the process of knocking down a wall to extend his living room when the wall collapsed and crashed through the floor onto his neighbour, Ken, in the flat below causing Ken severe injury and causing extensive damage to Ken's pictures. Ken's wife, Elizabeth, when she returned home from work, was so angry that she forced her way into Nick's flat and hit Nick over the head, causing him concussion.

Advise the parties of their criminal liability. How, if at all, would your advice differ if Nick had honestly believed that there was no risk of the wall collapsing and causing injury or damage?

(1)   Read the rubric

Although you are often asked, as in this case, to 'advise the parties' this does not necessarily mean advise *all* those mentioned in the scenario. Usually, there will be some characters who appear as mere victims and who, consequently have no criminal liability. In the situation under consideration, Ken, obviously, falls into this category. The parties to advise are, therefore, Nick and Elizabeth.

Notice the 'sting in the tail' and remember to highlight it in some fashion in order to ensure that it is not overlooked following detailed consideration of the liability of Nick and Elizabeth.

(2)   Read the scenario

Follow what should by now be the familiar procedure of reading through the scenario without paying to much attention to the various issues of law that may occur to you. Remember the purpose of this initial reading is simply to ascertain the facts and to note any areas of uncertainty or ambiguity.

Obviously, the question involves quite a wide range of offences, predominately against property and to a lesser extent against the person, together with a lack of certainty in relation to the *mens rea* of both parties. Somewhat less obvious is the uncertainty concerning ownership of the flat. Although we are told that it is Nick's flat, it may well be his in the sense that he has a right of occupation under the terms of a lease. This point will be of importance, as we shall see below, in relation to Nick's possible liability for criminal damage. Moreover, the ambiguous nature of the word 'forced' should be noted. This could imply an offence against property in the sense of 'forcing the door' or an offence against the person in the sense of Elizabeth 'forcing' or pushing her way into the flat. The facts are also 'open' in relation to the injury suffered by Nick, since 'concussion' could constitute either a life threatening condition or a relatively trivial harm depending upon its precise nature.

(3)   Identify the relevant offences and defences

Nick's liability

A consideration of Nick's possible liability in relation to both s 1(1) and s 1(2) of the Criminal Damage Act 1971 is called for in respect of his action of knocking down the wall in his flat. Additionally, there seems to be another s 1(1) criminal damage offence in relation to the extensively damaged pictures in the flat below.

Although the 'severe' injuries suffered by Ken would undoubtedly constitute the grievous bodily harm required for s 18 or s 20 of the Offences Against the Person Act 1861, there is uncertainty in relation to Nick's *mens rea* for these offences. Consequently, not only these two offences, but also the s 47 offence of an assault occasioning actual bodily harm should be considered.

Consideration would also have to be given to the defences of mistake in law and 'lawful excuse' within the scope of s 5(2)(a) of the Criminal Damage Act 1971, in relation to the damage done to the wall.

Elizabeth's liability

In forcing her way into Nick's flat Elizabeth may have incurred liability for burglary contrary to s 9(1)(a) of the Theft Act 1968 as well as for s 1(1) of the Criminal Damage Act 1971. However, if the force was used against the person rather than against property, for example, by pushing past Nick in order to gain entry, then common assault and battery as well as, possibly, s 47 of the Offences Against the Person Act 1861 would require consideration.

Since the concussion caused to Nick could possibly amount to a serious injury, Elizabeth's liability in relation to both the s 18 and s 20 grievous bodily harm offences should be considered. Assuming, as is perhaps more likely, that the concussion constitutes a lesser degree of harm, then liability for an assault occasioning actual bodily harm contrary to s 47 of the Offences Against the Person Act 1861 would also need to be discussed.

As noted above, there is a possibility that Elizabeth actually caused or intended to cause serious harm to Nick when she hit him over the head. In these circumstances she may become liable for a second burglary offence, this time contrary to s 9(1)(b) of the Theft Act 1968.

There do not seem to be any relevant defences that Elizabeth would be able to raise, although it would be worthwhile to briefly point out why self-defence and provocation are not available.

Figure 7 Summary of possible liability

PARTY	OFFENCE	COMMENTS	DEFENCE
Nick	Criminal damage (s 1(1) CDA 1971)	To the wall - not clear who owns the wall.	s 5(2)(b) CDA 1971 Mistake of law
	Criminal damage (s 1(2) CDA 1971)	To the wall	
	Criminal damage (s 1(1) CDA 1971)	To pictures	
	Wounding/GBH (s 18 OAP 1861)	*Mens rea* very unlikely	
	Wounding/GBH (s 20 OAP 1861)	*Mens rea* possible	
	Actual bodily harm (s 47 OAP 1861)	If Nick foresees causing fear	
Elizabeth	Burglary (s 9(1)(a) TA 1968)	If intention to cause serious harm at time of entry	
	Criminal damage (s 1(1) CDA 1971)	To door when 'forcing' entry	
	Assault/battery	If 'forcing' means pushing past Nick	
	Actual bodily harm (s 47 OAP 1861)	If Nick injured during 'forced' entry	
	Wounding/GBH (s 18 OAP 1861)	If 'concussion' a serious injury	
	Wounding/GBH (s 20 OAP 1861)	'Concussion' serious but no intention to do serious injury	
	Actual bodily harm (s 47 OAP 1861)	If 'concussion' not serious	
	Burglary (s 9(1)(b) TA 1968)	If Elizabeth causes or attempts to cause serious harm	

(4) Define the relevant offences

Remember to keep rigidly to the problem-solving procedure by following your identification of the various offences that each of the parties may possibly have committed with full or abbreviated common law or statutory definitions as appropriate. This will enable you to engage in the next stage of legal reasoning in a more focused manner. The offence definitions can then be readily analysed into *actus reus* and *mens rea* and these elements in turn broken down into their constituent concepts. Of course, at this stage there will often be a need for yet further definitions of these constituent concepts such as 'property', 'damage', 'entry' etc. However, you should remember to only engage in this most detailed level of definition if the concept is one which is problematic in the context of the scenario under consideration. For example, there is no need to spend much time defining 'property' in relation to either the wall or the pictures in this scenario since they both obviously constitute 'property' for the purpose of criminal damage. However, it is necessary to attempt a detailed definition of 'belonging to another' in relation to Nick's possible liability under s 1(1) of the Criminal Damage Act 1971, because we are informed that it is 'his flat' and, therefore, presumably, his wall.

(5) Engage in legal reasoning

Nick's liability

By knocking down the wall Nick might have incurred liability under s 1(1) of the Criminal Damage Act 1971. The definition of this offence can be stated in an abbreviated form as the intentional or reckless damaging or destroying of property belonging to another. Two of the elements of the *actus reus* are clearly satisfied since the wall both constitutes property and has been damaged. However, the third element requires that the damaged property 'belong to another' and this is somewhat more problematic as we have been informed that Nick is carrying out alterations to 'his flat'. If this means that Nick is the absolute owner of the flat then, obviously, the wall would not belong to another within the meaning of the section. Alternatively, bearing in mind that the vast majority of flats are held on leases, 'his flat' could simply mean that he is the one with a right of exclusive occupation. In these circumstances the wall may well be treated as belonging to another for the purposes of criminal damage.

The basic definition of belonging to another is provided in s 10(2) of the Criminal Damage Act 1971 which states:

'Property shall be treated for the purposes of this Act as belonging to any person:

(a) having the custody or control of it;

(b) having in it any proprietary right or interest (not being an equitable interest arising only from an agreement to transfer or grant an interest); or

(c) having a charge on it.'

It follows that if Nick is renting the flat, the landlord would either be the freeholder or a leaseholder, who is himself subletting, in either case he would clearly have a proprietary right within the meaning of paragraph (b) above. The flat would still 'belong to another', this time within the meaning of paragraph (c), if Nick was in the process of buying the freehold by means of a loan secured on the property. It seems, then, that although, the *actus reus* of criminal damage is somewhat problematic, it does appear likely to be eventually established within the terms of s 10(2)(b) or (c).

However, the *mens rea* is also problematic in the sense that Nick could argue that he honestly thought he had the right to demolish the wall under the terms of his lease. Of course, such structural alterations are nearly always prohibited, at least without the freeholder's consent, in leasehold agreements, but the point being made is that this mistake of law as to the rights contained in the lease could operate to negative the *mens rea* required for criminal damage. A similar denial of *mens rea* could be made by contending that Nick honestly believed that the property he was destroying was his own, and that he, therefore, lacked an intention to destroy property belonging to another. This could amount to another mistake of civil law as to the ownership of the property and is, perhaps, more likely to occur where Nick is purchasing the flat with the aid of a loan secured by a charge on the property. As we have seen, in such a situation the property would be treated as 'belonging to another' within the terms of s 10(2)(c) of the Criminal Damage Act 1971. Both the above arguments amount to a denial of *mens rea* based on mistakes of civil law.

It is, of course, well established that a mistake or ignorance of the criminal law cannot operate as a defence even where the mistake was quite reasonable and even where it was impossible for the defendant to know of the prohibition in question (*R v Bailey* (1800)). In contrast, a mistake of civil law may provide a defence to a criminal charge where the *actus reus* requires proof of a legal concept such as that of 'belonging to another' in relation to s 1(1) criminal damage. This is because the defendant will, lack *mens rea* if he is not intentional or reckless in relation to such an element of the *actus reus*. The point is well illustrated by the case of *R v Smith* (1974) where the defendant's conviction for criminal damage was quashed by the Court of Appeal, because he had honestly (although as a matter of civil law incorrectly) thought that the fittings he had removed from his rented flat belonged in law to him rather than his landlord. It follows that if Nick honestly, although not necessarily reasonably, believed that either he had a legal right to destroy the property or that the property belonged to him, then he would lack the requisite *mens rea*.

Nick could also argue that he had a 'lawful excuse' in that he honestly believed that the freeholder, or owner of the charge, would have consented to the alterations had they have known of them. Section 5(2)(a) of the Criminal Damage Act 1971 provides that a person is to be treated as having a lawful excuse if:

'At the time of the act or acts alleged to constitute the offence he believed that the person or persons whom he believed to be entitled to consent to the destruction of or damage to the property in question had so consented, or would have so consented to it if he or they had known of the destruction or damage and its circumstances.'

Section 5(3) further provides that it is immaterial whether such a belief is justified or not if it is honestly held. Clearly, Nick may well be able to claim 'lawful excuse' within the meaning of s 5(2)(a) in addition to the mistake of civil law defence discussed above.

In addition to the 'basic' offence contrary to s 1(1), it would also be necessary to consider Nick's liability in relation to the 'aggravated' offence under s 1(2) of the Criminal Damage Act 1971. Section 1(2) provides:

'A person who without lawful excuse destroys or damages any property, whether belonging to himself or another:

(a) intending to destroy or damage any property or being reckless as to whether any property would be destroyed or damaged; and

(b) intending by the destruction or damage to endanger the life of another or being reckless as to whether the life of another would be thereby endangered;

shall be guilty of an offence.'

Since there is no need for the purposes of this subsection for the property to belong to another the establishment of the *actus reus* appears relatively unproblematic. However, the 'aggravating' factor contained in paragraph (b), consisting of an intention to endanger life or recklessness as to whether this occurs, renders the *mens rea* somewhat problematic.

As there is no evidence in the scenario of an intention to endanger life our discussion of the *mens rea* will focus on whether Nick could be reckless in this respect. The type of recklessness required for criminal damage is that laid down in *MPC v Caldwell* (1982) and which can be given an abbreviated definition in terms of the conscious or unconscious taking of an obvious risk. The main difficulty for the prosecution would be to establish an 'obvious risk' in the objective sense of a risk that a reasonable person would have been aware of (*Elliot v C* (1983)). Obviously, on the facts given it is not possible to come to any firm conclusion as to whether a reasonable person would have foreseen the risk of the damaged property endangering life. Clearly, if the risk of endangerment to life was not 'obvious' in this sense then Nick will lack the *mens rea* for the offence. Alternatively, if the risk would be obvious to the reasonable person, Nick's liability would then depend on whether he consciously or unconsciously took that risk.

Once again we cannot be certain as to what is going on in Nick's mind when he destroyed the wall, but it is, on the basis of the known facts, rather unlikely that he was 'subjectively' reckless in the sense of being aware of a risk of endangering life and nevertheless deciding to take that risk. More probably he gave no thought to the risk to life that his actions created. If this is, indeed, the position, then Nick has unconsciously taken an obvious risk and is, therefore, reckless in the *Caldwell* sense. Of course, there is also the possibility that Nick did consider the risk of danger to life and concluded (eg because he thought the other flat was unoccupied) that there was no risk at all. This situation would constitute the 'lacuna' in the *Caldwell* definition of recklessness and would function to relieve him of liability (*Chief Constable of Avon and Somerset v Shimmen* (1986); *R v Reid* (1992)).

So far we have considered Nick's liability for criminal damage in relation to the wall of his flat, but there would also be the question of his liability regarding the damage done to Ken's flat and his pictures. The appropriate offence here would be criminal damage contrary to s 1(1) of the Criminal Damage Act 1971. Unlike our discussion of this offence concerning the wall, it appears that the *actus reus* is unproblematic in relation to the both the flat and the pictures. Evidently property belonging to another has been damaged and, equally evidently, the defences of mistake of civil law and 'lawful excuse' within the meaning of s 5(2) are not relevant here.

Since it appears very unlikely that Nick intended to cause damage to property belonging to another, our discussion of the necessary *mens rea* for the s 1(1) offence will once again focus on the concept of *Caldwell* type recklessness. Although we argued above, in relation to s 1(2), that a reasonable person would not have necessarily foreseen the risk of danger to life, it would appear far more easy for the prosecution to prove that a reasonable person would have foreseen the risk of damage to property belonging to another required for s 1(1). Assuming that such an 'obvious' risk is established, Nick's liability would then depend upon whether he consciously or unconsciously took that risk. Once again it is impossible to know what is going on in his mind at the relevant moment, but it would appear that he is much less likely to avoid liability on the basis of the 'lacuna' argument. After all, he is hardly likely to have considered the risk of damaging property belonging to another involved in knocking down a wall in an upstairs flat and concluded that there was *no risk at all*. Assuming that there is an obvious risk of damaging property belonging to another and that there is no scope for the 'lacuna' argument, then Nick would be liable for the s 1(1) offence.

As we are informed that Ken suffered 'severe' injury as a result of the wall crashing through into his flat, a discussion of Nick's possible liability in relation to s 18 and s 20 of the Offences Against the Person Act 1861 would be required. The s 18 offence is committed by a person who:

'... maliciously ... wound or cause grievous bodily harm ... with intent to do some grievous bodily harm ...'.

The causation element of the *actus reus* is unproblematic in the context of the scenario since we are informed that Nick caused the wall to collapse and that the collapsing wall caused the injuries to Ken. Similarly, there is little doubt that a 'severe' injury would satisfy the definition of grievous bodily harm as 'serious harm' put forward by the Court of Appeal in *R v Saunders* (1985).

Although, as we have seen, the *actus reus* appears unproblematic the same cannot be said of the necessary *mens rea* of intention to cause grievous bodily harm. Of course, on the basis of the facts provided it would seem extremely unlikely that Nick had a direct intention to cause serious harm, but it is just possible, although still very unlikely, that he did foresee the virtual certainty of such harm. Since we do not know what is going on in his mind all that can be said is that if he foresaw the virtual certainty of causing serious harm to someone when he demolished the wall then he would have committed the s 18 offence.

The s 20 offence appears more relevant to the situation described in the scenario. This consists of:

'... malicious wounding ...' or '...maliciously inflicting grievous bodily harm ...'.

Since it has been held that the word 'inflicting' does not necessarily imply the need for an assault, it would appear that the *actus reus* is the same as that for the s 18 offence (*R v Wilson* (1983)). As we noted above, the necessary elements of causation and grievous bodily harm would appear to be made out.

The *mens rea* required for this offence is denoted by the word 'malicious', a term which has been interpreted by the Court of Appeal in *R v Cunningham* (1957) as the conscious taking of an unjustified risk. When considering this definition it is vitally important to specify precisely what the 'unjustified risk' must relate to. This was clarified by Diplock LJ in the case of *R v Mowatt* (1967) as foresight of the risk of some physical harm. While we cannot be certain whether there would be an 'unjustified risk' of this kind, it is quite possible that a reasonable person would have recognised such a danger inherent in Nick's course of action. Assuming this to be the case, liability would then depend on whether Nick knowingly took that risk. Yet again we do not know what was in Nick's mind when he was demolishing the wall, but if, as seems likely, he was not subjectively conscious of the risk of causing physical harm, then, he would lack the requisite *mens rea* for the offence.

Although Nick may not have foreseen any risk of physical harm occurring to any other person, and hence lack the *mens rea* for the s 20 offence (*R v Sullivan* (1981)), he might possibly have foreseen that his actions would cause another to fear the infliction of such harm. In these circumstances he would have the necessary *mens rea* for an offence contrary to s 47 of the Offences Against the Person Act 1861. This offence can be simply defined as intentionally or recklessly committing an '... assault occasioning actual bodily harm ...'

The *actus reus*, therefore, consists of three elements: an assault, which in the context of s 47 includes a battery, causation and resulting actual bodily harm. It would seem that all these *actus reus* requirements are satisfied, Ken has suffered the infliction of a battery which has caused 'severe injury' let alone actual bodily harm. The fact that the battery was of an indirect nature would seem to be no bar to conviction (*R v Martin* (1881); *Scott v Shepard* (1773)).

The *mens rea* would be established assuming that Nick did, indeed, foresee the risk of causing another to fear the immediate infliction of unlawful violence (perhaps because he realised that the noise of demolition would cause just such fear in the residents of the flat below). However, if the 'assault' alleged by the prosecution took the form of a battery, Nick could argue that there was no correspondence of *actus reus* and *mens rea* since he caused a battery, but foresaw only the risk of causing fear. In terms of principle this would appear to be a sound argument, but it is suggested that in practice the courts may well tend to treat the *mens rea* of an assault and battery as interchangeable.

Elizabeth's liability

In forcing her way into Nick's flat Elizabeth may have committed an offence contrary to s 1(1) of the Criminal Damage Act 1971. Assuming that damage has actually been caused to the flat in order to gain entry, and the use of the word 'forced' tends to imply that it has, then all the *actus reus* requirements for this offence would be satisfied. Moreover, since the word 'forced' also implies purposeful action Elizabeth would seem to have caused the damage intentionally.

Elizabeth's liability for burglary contrary to s 9(1)(a) of the Theft Act 1968 should also be considered in relation to her forced entry. This offence is committed if a person 'enters any building or part of a building as a trespasser' with an intention to steal, inflict grievous bodily harm, rape or do any unlawful damage therein. Clearly, the *actus reus* requirements would all be satisfied; Elizabeth has entered part of a building and she is obviously a trespasser if she has to force her way in. However, the *mens rea* is somewhat more problematic in that the facts provided do not disclose her state of mind at the time of her entry. All that can be said here is that *if* Elizabeth did have an intention to cause grievous bodily harm at the time of entering Nick's flat then she would incur liability for burglary contrary to s 9(1)(a).

Of course, the above discussion has been based on the assumption that Elizabeth used force against property in order to gain entry to the flat. However, she could equally well have used force against the person for the same purpose. It would be a perfectly reasonable use of language to say that she 'forced' her way in by, pushing or shouldering her way past Nick. According to this interpretation of the scenario she may well have incurred liability for a common assault or battery. An assault is any act by which the defendant, intentionally or recklessly, causes the victim to apprehend immediate personal violence (*Fagan v MPC* (1969)). Given the fact that Elizabeth is not only 'angry', but also that she 'forced' her way into Nick's flat, Nick may well have feared the immediate infliction of unlawful violence. If this was, indeed, the case, then the *actus reus* of the offence would be made out. The *mens rea* would seem to be equally unproblematic in that she surely intended to cause fear or was at least reckless, in the *Cunningham* sense, as to this consequence of her actions.

In the somewhat unlikely event of Nick not being frightened there would almost certainly be liability arising in relation to a common battery. A battery is any act by which the defendant, intentionally or recklessly, inflicts unlawful personal violence upon the victim (*R v Rolfe* (1952). If Elizabeth has pushed or shouldered her way past Nick then the *actus reus*, consisting of a touching of another without consent, would undoubtedly be made out (*Faulkner v Talbot* (1981)). Moreover, as we noted above, the word 'forced' tends to imply purposeful action so the *mens rea* for this offence would also be satisfied.

If Nick suffered 'any hurt or injury likely to interfere with health or comfort' as a result of Elizabeth inflicting a battery on him by forcing her way into the flat then she would commit an offence contrary to s 47 of the Offences Against the Person Act 1861.

Elizabeth's liability in relation to her action of hitting Nick over the head and causing him concussion would also require consideration. The facts provided in the scenario are 'open' in two important respects here. Firstly, there is the problem of establishing the appropriate *actus reus*, since 'concussion' would certainly amount to actual bodily harm, but could conceivably amount to more serious harm. Secondly, as is so often the case, there is uncertainty concerning *mens rea* at the time the blow was struck. Given these uncertainties, a range of non-fatal offences, from s 18 grievous bodily harm to s 47 actual bodily harm should be considered.

Assuming both that the concussion did amount to a serious injury and that Elizabeth intended to do serious harm then she would incur liability under s 18. Indeed, there is some evidence in the scenario to suggest that Elizabeth did have such an intention, for example, we are informed that she hit Nick 'over the head' which implies the use of an object of some kind. This in turn may provide some evidence of the requisite intention to do grievous bodily harm.

Another possibility would be that the concussion amounted to 'serious harm', satisfying the *actus reus* requirement of grievous bodily harm (*R v Saunders* (1985)), but that Elizabeth lacked the necessary intent for the s 18 offence. In these circumstances she could be liable in relation to the s 20 offence of malicious wounding or causing grievous bodily harm. As we noted in our discussion of Nick's liability, the *mens rea* for this offence is denoted by the word 'malicious' which has been interpreted to mean the conscious taking of an unjustified risk of some physical harm (*R v Cunningham* (1957); *R v Mowatt* (1968)). It follows that if Elizabeth either intended any degree of physical harm, or foresaw the risk of causing some physical harm, she would have the requisite *mens rea*. Indeed, it somewhat unlikely that she could have hit someone over the head without foreseeing the risk of some harm, albeit only slight.

However, if the concussion did not amount to a serious injury, then liability in relation to an assault occasioning actual bodily harm contrary to s 47 of the Offences Against the Person Act 1861 would have to be considered. There would be no doubt that the *actus reus* requirements are all satisfied. The blow on the head would amount to a battery, which is included in the term 'assault'. Moreover, this blow has occasioned, or caused, actual bodily harm in the sense of any hurt or injury likely to interfere with the health or comfort of the victim (*R v Miller* (1954)).

The *mens rea* for the s 47 offence would seem to be as unproblematic as the *actus reus* since the blow to the head appears to have been struck intentionally. The House of Lords in *R v Savage* (1991) established that there is no need for the *mens rea* ,of intention or recklessness (of the *Cunningham* variety), to extend to the resulting actual bodily harm; all that is required is that it relates to the initial assault.

If Elizabeth either inflicted grievous bodily harm or attempted to do so when she hit Nick over the head then she might simultaneously have committed an offence of burglary contrary to s 9(1)(b) of the Theft Act 1968. This section provides that:

'A person is guilty of burglary if having entered any building or part of a building as a trespasser he steals or attempts to steal anything in the building or that part of it or inflicts or attempts to inflict on any person therein any grievous bodily harm.'

Somewhat curiously, it would seem that the infliction of grievous bodily harm under s 9(1)(b) does not have to constitute an offence, it merely requires the defendant to have inflicted or attempted to inflict grievous bodily harm upon the victim (*R v Jenkins* (1983)). Therefore, if either the concussion amounted to grievous bodily harm, or Elizabeth intended serious harm when she struck Nick, the offence conditions would be satisfied, assuming, of course, that her entry was as a trespasser.

The 'sting in the tail'

If Nick had honestly believed that there was no risk of the wall collapsing and causing injury or damage then he would not be reckless because such a mental state would amount to the 'loophole' or 'lacuna' in the definition of *Caldwell* recklessness recognised by the House of Lords in *R v Reid* (1992). This occurs where the defendant does consider whether there is a risk, but then, mistakenly, decides that there is no or, at most, a negligible risk. Nick neither unconsciously takes an obvious risk of the wall collapsing and causing injury or damage, because he has considered the risk, nor does he consciously take such risks since he decided that there was no risk.

Moreover, since Nick honestly believes that there is no risk of the wall collapsing and causing injury he will lack the foresight of some physical harm required for establishing the *mens rea* of *Cunningham* recklessness in relation to s 20 of the Offences Against the Person Act 1861.

Defences 5

Even where the defendant has caused an *actus reus* with the appropriate *mens rea* he will not always be liable, for there may be a valid defence available. In addition to particular defences which apply to certain crimes, there are general defences which can be raised in relation to all offences. The scenarios found in this chapter are designed to focus attention on both these types of defence as well as pleas such as 'automatism', 'mistake' and 'consent' which, although not defences in the strict sense, nevertheless, function as denials of *actus reus* or *mens rea*. Once again, you may find it beneficial to read through the relevant concise notes, contained in Chapter 8, before studying the following scenarios.

Scenario 8

Roger invited Jan, a total abstainer, to a party to be held at Roger's isolated country cottage. Roger believed that Jan had been given a lift to the party whereas in fact she had driven herself. Roger laced Jan's orange juice as a joke. Jan began to feel ill and decided to drive home. On her way home Jan overtook a car on a dangerous bend and crashed into a vehicle coming the other way, killing the driver. When Roger heard about the accident he was so shocked that he fell into a trance-like state during which he hit his girlfriend over the head with a garden gnome. When the police arrived Roger was found jumping up and down shouting 'a goblin, a goblin, I've killed a goblin'.

Discuss the criminal liability of the parties.

(1) Read the rubric

A fairly simple rubric requiring us to consider the liability of Roger and Jan.

(2) Read the scenario

Although we are asked to discuss the liability of Roger and Jan for various offences implicit in the scenario, the problem primarily focuses on defences such as intoxication, automatism and insanity. Once again, read through the scenario in order to gain an overview of the facts without worrying too much about the law at this stage. Remember to note areas of uncertainty where the facts are open to different interpretations. For example, we are not told with what substance Roger laces Jan's orange juice, nor precisely how ill Jan feels. Finally, as is often the case in criminal problems, the extent of the injuries suffered by the victim, Roger's girlfriend, are not specified.

(3)   Identify the relevant offences and defences

Roger's liability

Roger's action in lacing Jan's drink calls for a discussion of several possible offences. These would include maliciously administering a noxious substance so as thereby to endanger life contrary to s 23 of the Offences Against the Person Act 1861, or, alternatively, maliciously administering a noxious substance, with intent to injure aggrieve or annoy, contrary to s 24 of the same Act. In addition, the possibility of liability for criminal damage under s 1(2) of the Criminal Damage Act 1971 should be considered.

By causing Jan to become intoxicated, Roger may incur liability as an accessory to 'motor manslaughter' or causing death by dangerous driving as well as criminal damage contrary to s 8 of the Accessories and Abettors Act 1861.

Finally, of course, there should be a discussion of Roger's liability in relation to the attack on his girlfriend. Although the uncertainty regarding the seriousness of the injuries sustained would normally prompt a consideration of the full range of non-fatal offences, on this occasion, given Roger's apparent mental state, our attention should primarily focus on the defences that might be available to him.

Jan's liability

Obviously, the relevant offences as far as Jan is concerned would be either 'motor manslaughter' or causing death by dangerous driving together with criminal damage to the vehicles involved in the accident. However, attention should concentrate on the defences of automatism and intoxication as it appears that Jan could lack mental responsibility for her actions.

Figure 8 Summary of possible liability

PARTY	OFFENCE	COMMENTS	DEFENCE
Roger	Administering noxious substance (s 23 OAP 1861)	Life must be endangered	
	Administering noxious substance (s 24 OAP 1861)	Must be ulterior intention	
	Criminal damage (s 1(2) CDA 1971)	By damaging the orange juice	
	Accomplice (s 8 AAA 1861)	Accessory to 'motor manslaughter' or causing death by dangerous driving and criminal damage	
	Wounding/GBH (s 20 OAP 1861)	Extent of injuries uncertain	Automatism Insanity
	Actual bodily harm (s 47 OAP 1861)		Automatism Insanity
Jan	Motor manslaughter, causing death by dangerous driving (s 1 RTA 1988)	Maybe 'lacuna'	Automatism Intoxication
	Criminal damage (s 1(2) CDA 1971)	To vehicles	Automatism Intoxication

(4) Define the relevant offences

By this stage it will have become, hopefully, second nature to commence your discussion of the various offences by providing a full, or, if possible, abbreviated definition, of the relevant offences.

(5) Engage in legal reasoning

Roger's liability

By lacing Jan's orange juice Roger may have committed several offences. One such possibility would be 'maliciously administering a noxious substance so as to endanger life, or inflict grievous bodily harm ...' contrary to s 23 of the Offences Against the Person Act 1861.

One element of the *actus reus* appears unproblematic since leaving a noxious substance for the victim to take up will amount to 'administering', provided it is swallowed and taken into the stomach (*Harley* (1830); *Cadman* (1825)). However, the position is not quite so clear cut in relation to whether a 'noxious substance' has been administered. Although there is uncertainly as to what substance the drink was laced with, the fact that Jan is a 'total abstainer' and that Roger is motivated by the desire to play a joke on her tend to suggest that alcohol was used. In *R v Marcus* (1981) 'noxious' was broadly interpreted as anything which if administered in sufficient quantities would injury, aggrieve or annoy. Somewhat paradoxically, the meaning of this element of the *actus reus*, therefore, seems to depend, at least to some extent, on the intention of the person administering the substance. Since Jan is a *total abstainer* and has been made to feel ill it seems reasonable to assume both that Roger intended to annoy and that she actually has been aggrieved or annoyed, if not injured. In these circumstances, it could be argued that the unknown quantity of, presumably, alcohol put into her orange juice would almost certainly amount to a 'noxious substance'.

Finally, as regards the *actus reus* of s 23, it would be necessary to prove that Jan's life has been endangered, or that she suffered the infliction of grievous bodily harm, as a consequence of the administration. In this respect, s 23 is a 'result crime', requiring proof that the defendant's action caused the prohibited consequence. This can be resolved by applying the so-called 'but for' test; but for Roger's action of lacing the drink would Jan's life have been endangered? It seems likely that Jan's life was endangered by the crash and that this would not have occurred *but for* Roger's action. Assuming that causation in *fact* could be established in this way, it would then be necessary to deal with the issue of whether Roger's action was a cause in *law* of the endangerment. This will, essentially, depend on whether the endangerment to life was a reasonably foreseeable consequence of what the defendant did. It may well be the case that a reasonable person, in the knowledge that the victim is a total abstainer and that the party is held in an isolated location, would foresee that life could be endangered as a consequence of lacing the drink. If this argument is accepted, then the *actus reus* of the s 23 offence would be made out.

If under s 23 the only *mens rea* required is intention or recklessness as to the administration of the noxious substance then, since it seems clear that there was such an intention to lace the drink, Roger would have the necessary mental element for the offence. However, if the *mens rea* must also extend to the endangerment of life or the infliction of grievous bodily harm, then liability would be more problematic as Roger's belief that Jan was not intending to drive home may well mean that he did not consciously take such a risk. Whether the *mens rea* does actually extend in this way to the second part of the *actus reus* is not clear on the basis of the present authorities, but it would seem unlikely, particularly in view of the way the House of Lords has resolved a similar issue in relation to s 47 of the Offences Against the Person Act 1861 (*R v Savage* (1991)).

Alternatively, liability in relation to maliciously administering a noxious substance with an intention to injure, aggrieve, or annoy contrary to s 24 of the Offences Against the Person Act 1861 should also be considered. The *actus reus* of this offence is the same as that for s 23 except that there is no need for the victim's life to have been endangered or for the infliction of grievous bodily harm. This being the case, bearing in mind our earlier arguments concerning 'administration' and 'noxious substance' it would seem that the establishment of the *actus reus* would be relatively unproblematic.

The *mens rea* for the s 24 offence consists of the intentional or reckless administration of a noxious substance, but, unlike s 23, an ulterior intent to injure, aggrieve or annoy is also required.

As we have already noted, there seems little doubt that Roger intended to administer the noxious substance, so the only remaining issue is whether or not he also had the requisite ulterior intent. The nature of this ulterior intent was considered by the House of Lords in *R v Hill* (1986) where it was stated that the matter had to be approached by looking at the object that the defendant had in mind. To keep a pilot awake by plying him with stimulants so that he could safely land an aircraft would not involve the commission of an offence, whereas to deprive him of sleep for the purposes of interrogation might well do so. Similarly, it was suggested that to keep a child awake in order to greet the arrival of a relative late at night, or view a fireworks display would fall outside s 24. When we look at Roger's motives it seems clear that he is administering the noxious substance in order to play a joke. However, given that Jan is a total abstainer, surely he realises that she is likely to be extremely annoyed when she realises what has happened. It, therefore, appears that Roger will satisfy both the *actus reus* and the *mens rea* requirements for the s 24 offence.

As well as the above 'poisoning' offences, Roger's liability for criminal damage to the orange juice ought also to be considered. Since the party is given by Roger, the orange juice probably belongs to him, consequently there is unlikely to be any liability for the basic offence of criminal damage contrary to s 1(1). Indeed, this could only occur if Roger damaged the drink by lacing it *after* ownership had been transferred to Jan and this seems rather unlikely. However, there is no need for property to belong to another in relation to s 1(2) of the Criminal Damage Act 1971 which provides:

'A person who without lawful excuse destroys or damages any property, whether belonging to himself or another:

(a) intending to destroy or damage any property or being reckless as to whether any property would be destroyed or damaged; and

(b) intending by the destruction or damage to endanger life of another or being reckless as to whether the life of another would be thereby endangered;

shall be guilty of an offence.'

It would appear that the *actus reus*, of destroying or damaging property, is satisfied. Clearly the orange juice would come within the definition property, provided by s 10(1) of the Criminal Damage Act, as of a 'tangible nature, whether real or personal'. Moreover, it can be argued that the property has been damaged because the purpose of a soft drink in a party setting is surely to provide an alcohol-free drink. The illicit lacing of the orange juice would, thus, constitute the kind of 'functional derangement' envisaged by the court in *Samuel v Stubbs* (1972) as one possible defining feature of criminal damage.

Although, given Roger's apparent belief that Jan is not going to drive home, it would be difficult for the prosecution to establish an intention to endanger life, proof of recklessness would suffice for s 1(2). The recklessness in question is the 'objective' or *Caldwell* type which imposes liability upon the defendant if his conduct:

(1) creates an obvious risk of endangering life by damaging property; and

(2) he either;

    (a)   gives no thought to the possibility of there being any such risk; or

    (b)   recognising that there is some risk goes on to take it.

Arguably, the requirement of an 'obvious' risk seems to have been satisfied in that a reasonable person might have appreciated that there was a risk that the adulterated orange juice might cause endangerment to life. Nevertheless, Roger's situation may fall outside both the above conditions in that he appears to have considered the risk, but then decided, because of his belief that Jan was going to obtain a lift home, that there was no risk to life at all. This is, of course, the *lacuna* referred to by Mustill LJ in *R v Reid* (1992) when he said that one who recognised the existence of a risk but who concluded there was none (or that the risk was negligible or less than serious) must be acquitted.

There seems little prospect of Roger incurring liability as a principal in relation to any of the offences that may have been committed by Jan. This is because Jan can hardly be regarded as an innocent agent of Roger as she does seem to have been aware of her actions at the time of the collision. However, by causing her to become intoxicated, Roger could incur liability as an accessory to criminal damage and 'motor manslaughter' or causing death by dangerous driving. Section 8 of the Accessories and Abettors Act 1861 provides that:

'Whosoever shall aid, abet, counsel, or procure the commission ... (of an offence) ... shall be liable to be tried, indicted, and punished as a principal offender.'

Roger's action of lacing the orange juice could amount to the *actus reus* of this offence by procuring the commission of both criminal damage and the motor manslaughter or causing death by dangerous driving. Indeed, the facts are somewhat similar to those in *Attorney General's Reference No 1 of 1975* (1975) where the accused had surreptitiously laced a friend's drink knowing the friend would be driving home. In the Court of Appeal, Lord Widgery CJ said that to procure meant to produce by endeavour and that the defendant's actions were clearly capable of amounting to procuring the offence of drunken driving.

However, establishing the necessary *mens rea* for accessorial liability would appear to be rather more problematic in relation to Roger's situation. Not only must the defendant have intended to do the acts of assisting, encouraging or procuring the commission of the crime, but also he must have contemplated the *type* of offence that would be committed by the principal (*R v Bainbridge* (1960)). In contrast to the defendant in the aforementioned case of *Attorney General's Reference No 1 of 1975* (1975), Roger believed that Jan would have a lift home and, therefore, would not contemplate the commission of any of the relevant offences by her.

 Be extremely cautious when the scenario appears to resemble a decided case. Usually, in an attempt to catch out the student with only superficial understanding, the examiner will have made a slight alteration to the facts which significantly affects the legal position.

In relation to the 'open' nature of the scenario concerning the extent of the injuries suffered by Roger's girlfriend, there would seem to be three possibilities:

(1) that she dies within a year and a day of the injury;

(2) that she suffers a wound or serious injury; and

(3) that she survives the incident with no or only minor injury.

Given Roger's apparent lack of intent the possible areas of liability would appear to be manslaughter, wounding or inflicting grievous bodily harm or an assault occasioning actual bodily harm. However, since Roger's liability in relation to each of these eventualities depends on whether or not he would be able to succeed with the defences of automatism or insanity, a detailed consideration of the various *actus reus* requirements can be avoided.

The phrase 'trance like state' suggests that when Roger hits his girlfriend over the head with the garden gnome he is not engaging in consciously willed conduct and would, therefore, be able to escape liability. As Lord Denning stated in *Bratty v Attorney General for Northern Ireland* (1963):

'No act is punishable if it is done involuntarily and an involuntary act in this context - some people nowadays prefer to speak of it as 'automatism' - means an act which is done by the muscles without any control by the mind.'

It follows that if Roger can produce some evidence, preferable of a medical nature, that he was acting as an automaton at the time of the attack, and the prosecution are unable to conclusively contradict this evidence, he will have a complete defence to any offence charged and be entitled to a verdict of not guilty.

However, Roger's subsequent behaviour in jumping up and down and shouting 'I've killed a goblin' tends to suggest some form of mental illness rather than involuntary conduct *per se*. Where the defendant adduces evidence of automatism, the prosecution are permitted to counter this by evidence that the condition giving rise to the automatism is 'a disease of the mind' and that the defendant is consequently entitled to only a qualified acquittal on grounds of insanity (*Bratty v Attorney General for Northern Ireland*). In these circumstances the judge must make one of a number of orders which could include a hospital order with or without restrictions on discharge (s 5 of the Criminal Procedure (Insanity) Act 1964, as substituted by the Criminal Procedure (Insanity and Unfitness to Plead) Act 1991 Schedule 1). Although any psychiatric evidence would be considered by the court, whether or not Roger's condition amounts to a 'disease of the mind' is essentially a question of law.

The expression 'disease of the mind' has been liberally interpreted by the courts to include arterial sclerosis, a condition which restricts the blood supply to brain and can cause 'blackouts' (*R v Kemp* (1957)), epilepsy (*R v Sullivan* (1984)), schizophrenia and diabetes (*R v Hennessy* (1989)). Indeed, in *Bratty v Attorney General for Northern Ireland*, Lord Denning said that any condition which 'manifested itself in violence and is prone to recur is a disease of the mind'. This pragmatic approach enables the courts to exercise control over those who, although not responsible for the harm caused, are, nevertheless, perceived to be a danger to society. It is this sort of policy consideration which provides the rationale for the so-called 'internal/external' doctrine laid down by the Court of Appeal in *R v Quick* (1973) and affirmed by the House of Lords in *R v Sullivan*. According to this doctrine if the malfunctioning of the mind is caused by a factor external to the body then the condition does not constitute a disease of the mind and the defendant is entitled to acquitted on grounds of automatism. If, on the other hand, the cause is said to internal then this would amount to a disease of the mind and the appropriate verdict would be not guilty by reason of insanity.

Whether Roger is entitled to a complete acquittal on grounds of automatism or a not guilty verdict by reason of insanity, maybe with an accompanying hospital order, would depend upon whether the cause of his mental condition was internal or external. At first glance it would appear that Roger's mental condition was the result of an external event; the psychological blow of hearing about the fatal accident that Jan was involved in. However, in the Canadian case of *Rabey* (1977) it was argued that a 'dissociative state' resulting from a 'psychological blow' was evidence of insanity rather than automatism since 'the ordinary stresses and disappointments of life which are the common lot of mankind do not constitute an external cause ...'. It seems somewhat unlikely that a 'normal' person would have reacted to the admittedly shocking news of the accident in the way that Roger did. It can, therefore, be argued that the exceptional effect which the news of the accident had on him must have had its source in his psychological or emotional make up. Of course, if this line of argument is accepted, then the cause of his behaviour would be internal rather than external and as such would result in the not guilty by reason of insanity verdict.

Jan's liability

Several offences could possibly have been committed as a result of the fatal accident between the cars. Obviously, the other vehicle involved in the accident will have sustained damage so the *actus reus* requirements of criminal damage contrary to s 1(1) of the Criminal Damage Act 1971 will have been satisfied. As, indeed, will those of s 1(2) of the same Act. Further, since there has been a fatality, there could be a charge of either 'motor manslaughter' or causing death by dangerous driving. However, establishing the *mens rea* for these offences is likely to prove somewhat more problematic in that as Jan appeared unwell/intoxicated at the time of the accident she may claim that she was not responsible for her actions. As we have seen, the most attractive argument from the defence point of view would be to claim that because of the effect of the alcohol on the central nervous system Jan was in a state of automatism at the time of the accident. If this argument were to succeed Jan would be found not guilty of all the offences arising out of the collision. However, there would seem to be, at least, two difficulties with establishing automatism in the circumstances of this particular case.

The first difficulty stems from a line of authority which suggests that there must be a *total* loss of control for the defence to succeed. In *Bratty v Attorney General*, Lord Denning said that automatism was confined to acts done while unconscious and to spasms, reflex actions and convulsions. Similarly, in *Broome v Perkins* (1987) the defendant was held guilty of driving without due care and attention, though in a hypoglycaemic state, because there was evidence that his mind had still been responding to 'gross stimuli', and that, therefore, his body had not been acting totally without the control of his mind. In *Attorney General's Reference No 2 of 1992* (1993) it was, likewise, held that impaired, reduced or partial control by the defendant would not found a defence of automatism. A total loss of voluntary control would be required. On the basis of these authorities it could be argued that if there was evidence that Jan was conscious that she was driving, albeit not fully conscious, the defence would fail. Nevertheless, there seems to be an alternative line of authority which would support the proposition that automatism may exist even though the condition of the defendant does not involve a total loss of control. According to this reading of the cases, an 'effective' loss of control resulting from *impaired* consciousness would suffice to found the defence (*R v Charlson* (1955); *R v Kemp* (1957); *R v T* (1990); *R v Burgess* (1991)).

A second problem stems from the principle that automatism will be no defence to crimes of 'basic intent', such as criminal damage and manslaughter, if the defendant was at fault for inducing the autonomic state in the first place (*R v Lipman* (1970)). Of course, Jan was not at fault for inducing the automatic state consequent upon the involuntary consumption of alcohol, but her fault in deciding to drive even though she knew she was feeling unwell may be sufficient to found liability under ordinary principles of responsibility (*Kay v Butterworth* (1945)). The key issue here would seem to be the question of just how unwell she felt. If is was clearly unreasonable for her to drive in such a condition then the 'obvious risk' required to establish the *Caldwell* recklessness necessary for both criminal damage and motor manslaughter would be made out (*Elliot v C* (1983); *R v Seymour* (1983)). Similarly, if she is charged with causing death by dangerous driving contrary to s 1 of the Road Traffic Act 1988 (as substituted by s 1 of the Road Traffic Act 1991) any evidence of prior fault would be likely to negate the defence of automatism.

Since, as we have seen, automatism may prove difficult to establish, the alternative defence of intoxication should also be considered. The general rule, following the decision of the House of Lords in *DPP v Majewski* (1977), is that intoxication will normally only be available as a defence to crimes of specific intent. As it is Jan's liability in relation to the basic intent crimes of criminal damage, motor manslaughter and causing death by dangerous driving which is under consideration, it would appear that intoxication would be no defence. However, the *Majewski* rule only applies to cases of *voluntary* intoxication and the circumstances appertaining to Jan provide an example of *involuntary* intoxication.

The law relating to involuntary intoxication appears to be narrowly defined in that a person who knew she was drinking alcohol could not claim that the resulting intoxication was involuntary merely because she underestimated the quantity or the strength of the drink (*R v Allen* (1988)). Of course, this principle would provide no bar to a defence of involuntary intoxication in Jan's case because she believed that she was merely drinking orange juice. It seems, then, that the rule in *Majewski* would not apply and that involuntary intoxication could be raised as a defence even to crimes of basic intent. This appears to be logical since the person who voluntarily becomes intoxicated is regarded as being to blame for his condition and his liability is founded on this prior fault, but the person who becomes involuntarily intoxicated is not responsible for his condition (*R v Hardie* (1984)). Somewhat surprising involuntary intoxication may provide a good defence even where the defendant forms the *mens rea* for the crime in question, provided there is evidence that he would not have done so but for the intoxication (*R v Kingston* (1993)). On this basis it is submitted that Jan may well succeed with the defence of involuntary intoxication.

Scenario 9

Richard falsely told Maureen, a student, that he was a criminal law examiner and that he would make sure that she obtained an especially high mark in her finals if she agreed to sleep with him. Maureen agreed and suggested that they go to the cinema before returning to her flat.

During the film Richard left his seat to buy ice-creams for himself and Maureen. In the dark Richard returned to the wrong seat. He put his hand on what he believed to be Maureen's thigh only to be punched on the nose by Keith who resented what he took to be Richard's homosexual advances.

Having regained his correct seat, Richard found that Maureen was suffering from an uncontrollable attack of hick-ups. She told him to 'do something about it' at which point he stuffed the ice-cream down the front of her dress. Maureen was so startled that she instinctively recoiled and bumped her head on the cinema wall.

Back at her flat, Maureen told Richard that she would like to be tied up and made love to. Richard did as she requested.

When Maureen subsequently discovered that Richard was not a criminal law examiner, but merely an administrative assistant, she claimed that she had been the victim of a 'date rape'.

Discuss the criminal liability of Richard and Keith.

(1) Read the rubric

A fairly straightforward rubric with the liability of two parties to consider and no 'sting in the tail'.

(2) Read the scenario

When the facts of a problem appear relatively unambiguous, as do those of the present scenario, the wary student would be well advised to expect compensating complexity or uncertainty in the relevant law. Even at this stage, where we should be mainly concerned with the facts, it will be apparent that the issue of consent is going to be of major significance to any legal analysis of the situation.

(3) Identify the relevant offences and defences

Richard's liability

Both blackmail and obtaining services by deception ought to be considered in relation to the first sentence of the scenario, if only to explain why Richard is unlikely to be liable for these offences. Once in the cinema, Richard's liability for inflicting a battery on Keith and an assault occasioning actual bodily harm on Maureen ought both to be considered. Obviously, the defence of consent will be of relevance here. Additionally, there is the easily missed possibility of criminal damage to Maureen's dress.

Richard's activities in Maureen's flat would require a discussion of battery, possibly an assault occasioning actual bodily harm and rape. However, the key issue in relation to all these offences will be, yet again, the availability of the defence of consent.

Keith's liability

Keith's action in punching Richard on the nose would necessitate a consideration of battery and an assault occasioning actual bodily harm contrary to s 47 of the Offences Against the Person Act 1861. Obviously, consideration should be given to the availability of the common law defence of self-defence and the alternative defence of using reasonable force to prevent crime contained in s 3(1) of the Criminal Law Act 1967.

Figure 9   Summary of possible liability

PARTY	OFFENCE	COMMENTS	DEFENCE
Richard	Blackmail (s 21 TA 1969)	No view to gain	
	Deception (s 1(1) TA 1978)	No understanding that payment will be made	
	Incitement	Implicit incitement doubtful	
	Conspiracy (s 1(1) CLA 1977)	Implicit agreement doubtful	
	Battery	On Keith	Mistake/consent
	Battery	On Maureen	Consent
	Actual bodily harm (s 47 OAP 1861)	On Maureen	Consent
	Criminal damage (s 1(1) CDA 1971)	To Maureen's dress	
	Battery	By tying Maureen	Consent
	Actual bodily harm (s 47 OAP 1861)	If hurt or injured	Consent
	Rape		Consent
Keith	Assault and battery	On Richard	Self-defence (s 3(1) CLA 1967)
	Actual bodily harm (s 47 OAP 1861)	If hurt or injured	Self-defence (s 3(1) CLA 1967)

(4)   Define the relevant offences

Although the facts provided in the scenario will lead us to consider defences such as self-defence and consent in some detail, nevertheless, it is important to commence your discussion of the liability of the parties by defining the offences that they could have committed. In this way your consideration of the relevant defences will be located in the context of particular offences. As we shall see, a defence might prove successful in relation to one offence, but not in relation to another. Any attempt to 'skip over' this definition stage could well result in the student tripping flat on their face. As usual the relevant definitions are provided at the commencement of each stage of the legal reasoning processes below.

(5)   Engage in legal reasoning

Richard's liability

At first sight, Richard's action in falsely representing himself as a criminal law examiner and offering Maureen a high mark in her finals in return for sexual favours seems unlikely to involve him in any criminal liability. However, it would be necessary to briefly explain why the offences that most readily spring to mind in this connection, blackmail and obtaining services by deception, are not appropriate.

Section 21(1) of the Theft Act 1968 provides:

'A person is guilty of blackmail if, with a view to gain for himself or another or with intent to cause loss to another, he makes any unwarranted demand with menaces ...'

It seems apparent that one of the necessary elements of the *actus reus*, that of 'menaces' is lacking in the present situation. After all, if Maureen refuses to comply with Richard's request all that he seems to implicitly intend is to allow her examination paper to be marked accurately. Moreover, the *mens rea* requirement that the demand be made by the defendant with a view to gain for himself or another, or with intent to cause loss to another is hardly likely to be satisfied. This is because s 34(2)(a) of the Theft Act 1968 provides that:

' ... "gain" and "loss" are to be construed as extending only to gain or loss in money or other property ...'.

Clearly, the demand is made in this case with a view to obtaining sexual favours rather than money or other property.

Similarly, Richard is unlikely to have any liability in relation to the offence of obtaining services by deception contrary to s 1(1) of the Theft Act 1978 which simply provides that:

'A person who by any deception dishonestly obtains services from another shall be guilty of an offence.'

Although one element of the *actus reus* appears to be satisfied in that there has plainly been a 'deception', it seems unlikely that the sexual favours which Richard requested would amount to a 'service' within the meaning of the Act. While there is nothing to expressly exclude acts which are contrary to morality or public policy, s 1(2) does require the relevant act to be done 'on the understanding that the benefit has been or will be paid for'. Although 'payment' may be said to describe any of the ways in which an obligation may be discharged, it is submitted that the promise to provide especially high examination marks would strain the ordinary commercial meaning of the word too far. According to this view Richard would not have obtained a 'service' by deception.

Bearing in mind that Maureen may well use her inflated qualification to gain employment, there is the possibility of Richard being liable for inciting Maureen to obtain a pecuniary advantage by deception contrary to s 16 of the Theft Act 1968. It seems clear that incitement may be implied as well as express, for example, to advertise an article for sale, representing that it may be used to do an act which is an offence, is an incitement to commit that offence (*Invicta Plastics Ltd v Clare* (1976)). However, the mere intention to manufacture and sell a device which has no function other than one involving the commission of an offence is not an intention to incite the commission of that offence (*R v James and Ashford* (1985)). It is submitted that the situation presently under consideration more closely resembles the latter than the former case. Surely, a suggestion that Maureen should obtain an inflated class of degree is not, on its own, an implicit suggestion that she commits the s 16 offence.

For somewhat similar reasons it seems unlikely that there could be a conspiracy between Richard and Maureen to obtain a pecuniary advantage by deception. In short, it seems to be stretching the facts too far to suggest that there is an implicit agreement between the parties that Maureen obtain employment on the basis of her falsified qualification.

Richard's liability for battery would have to be considered in relation to his action of putting his hand on Keith's thigh in the cinema. A battery, which is now to be charged as a statutory offence contrary to s 39 of the Criminal Justice Act 1988, can be defined as any act by which the defendant intentionally or recklessly inflicts unlawful personal violence upon another (*R v Rolfe* (1952)). The 'violence' required is minimal as Lane LCJ said, in *Faulkner v Talbot* (1981), a battery:

'... is any intentional touching of another person without the consent of that person and without lawful excuse. It need not necessarily be hostile, or rude, or aggressive ...'.

Both the *actus reus* and the *mens rea* requirements appear to be satisfied as there certainly seems to have been an intentional touching. However, it is the essence of a battery that the infliction of violence must have been without the consent of the victim. Although it is clear that Keith did not consent to the touching, Richard could still argue, because he thought Keith was Maureen, that he mistakenly believed the victim to be consenting.

The leading case of *DPP v Morgan* (1976) decided that mistake is a defence where it prevents the defendant from having the *mens rea* for the crime in question. Where the law requires, as in the case of a battery, intention or reckless-ness, a mistake, whether reasonable or not, which precludes both states of mind will excuse. It follows that an honest mistake as to the consent of the victim will afford a defence, regardless of whether the mistake is one that the reasonable per-son would have made or not (*R v Kimber* (1983); *Beckford v R* (1988)). If Richard honestly believed that Maureen would have consented to his touching her in this way and if he had honestly believed that Keith was Maureen, then it would appear that these mistakes would negate his *mens rea* for the battery.

Similar issues would be of relevance in relation to Richard's action of stuff-ing the ice-cream down the front of Maureen's dress. Clearly, this is a touching with the potential to amount to another battery. Again both the *actus reus* and the *mens rea* requirements initially appear to be satisfied in that there has been an intentional infliction of 'violence', albeit of a minimal nature. Yet, once more, Richard will be able to raise the defences of consent, or, perhaps, rather more likely, a mistaken belief in the consent of the victim. It seems, on the basis of the facts, rather unlikely that Richard would succeed with the first of these defences. Notwithstanding that Maureen probably did consent to being fright-ened, or possibly even to being slapped on the back, in order to relieve her of hick-ups, it is somewhat improbable that she would have consented to the rela-tively drastic action involving the ice-cream. Richard would, therefore, seem to be on firmer ground in relation to the second defence of honest belief in the con-sent of the victim. Although, as we have already noted, the belief in the victim's consent must be honest, but need not be reasonable, it should, nevertheless, be remembered that the more unlikely the defendant's mistake, the less likely the jury will be to believe that he honestly made it.

As the infliction of the battery by Richard seems to have resulted in Maureen suffering a hurt or injury the question of liability in relation to an assault occa-sioning actual bodily harm contrary to s 47 of the Offences Against the Person Act 1861 should also be considered. All the elements of the *actus reus*; an assault (a term which includes a battery) and resulting actual bodily harm seem to be present. Moreover, the *mens rea* appears to be present, since all that is required is intention or recklessness in relation to the initial 'assault', not necessarily extending to the consequent actual bodily harm (*R v Savage* (1991)).

Whether or not Richard would be able to succeed with the defence of honest belief in the consent of the victim appears to be somewhat problematic, even if we assume that he did have such a belief. This is because of the House of Lords decision in *R v Brown and Others* (1993) where convictions of sado-masochistic homosexual men, under s 47 and s 20 of the Offences Against the Person Act 1861, were upheld despite the fact that the acts were done with consent in pri-vate. The majority of their Lordships (Lords Mustill and Slynn dissenting) con-tinued to regard consent as a defence to common assault, battery and indecent assault, but held that a person cannot effectively consent to the *deliberate* inflic-

103

tion of *bodily harm*, except in recognised cases, such as boxing. Consent to the *risk* of bodily harm appears to be another matter, unaffected by *Brown*. In relation to s 47 it seems, then, provided that the defendant's *mens rea* does not extend beyond the initial 'assault' to the consequent actual bodily harm, that consent could be a defence. Consent would also seem to be a valid defence even where the *mens rea* does extend to the resulting bodily harm, providing it takes the form of recklessness rather than intention. Applying this interpretation of the decision in *Brown* to Richard's action it could be argued that since he does not *deliberately* inflict bodily harm on Maureen his honest belief in her consent would found a valid defence.

It also seems Richard might be liable for criminal damage to Maureen's dress contrary to s 1(1) of the Criminal Damage Act 1971, which provides that:

'A person who without lawful excuse destroys or damages any property belonging to another intending to destroy or damage any such property or being reckless as to whether any such property would be destroyed or damaged shall be guilty of an offence.'

The three elements of the *actus reus* would all seem to be satisfied; the dress will have been damaged since it will almost certainly require cleaning, it would clearly constitute 'property', and, obviously, it belongs to another. In relation to the *mens rea* there seems little doubt that Richard either had an 'oblique intention' to damage the dress in that he foresaw this as a virtual certainty or he was reckless in that he consciously or unconsciously took an obvious risk that it would be damaged. Once again there are two possible defences; that Maureen consented or that he honestly believed that she consented. As we have argued above, while Maureen may well have consented to being frightened, it is somewhat unlikely that she would have consented to the damage to her dress. In relation to criminal damage, the second defence of honest belief in the victim's consent is contained in s 5(2)(a) of the 1971 Act, which provides:

'At the time of the act or acts alleged to constitute the offence he believed that the person or persons whom he believed to be entitled to consent to the destruction of or damage to the property in question had so consented, or would have so consented to it if he or they had known of the destruction or damage and its circumstances.'

Section 5(3) further provides that it is immaterial whether a belief is justified or not if it is honestly held. So, once again, Richard will have a good defence if he can convince the court that he honestly believed that Maureen would have consented to the damage to her dress. It is suggested that this is likely to prove a more difficult task than convincing them that he honestly believed that she had consented to a battery.

It follows from our earlier discussion of the leading case of *Brown* that Richard will be able to successfully raise the twin defences of consent and honest belief in the victim's consent in relation to his action of tying-up Maureen.

All that seems to have occurred is a common battery and, as we have seen, consent still remains a valid defence to this offence, even in situations of indecency (*R v Brown and Others* (1993)). Even if some injury is caused to Maureen, perhaps by ropes grazing her skin, the defence would still seem to be available as this is not the *deliberate* infliction of bodily harm.

Finally, Richard's liability for the alleged rape of Maureen should be considered. This offence is given a statutory basis by s 1(1) of The Sexual Offences Act 1956 which simply provides that: 'It is an offence for a man to rape a woman.' However, it is s 1(1) of the Sexual Offences (Amendment) Act 1976 which provides a definition of the offence by providing that a man commits rape if:

'(a) he has unlawful sexual intercourse with a woman who at the time of the intercourse does not consent to it; and

(b) at the time he knows that she does not consent to the intercourse or he is reckless as to whether she consents to it.'

Of course, the crucial issue in the present case would be whether fraud on the part of Richard could have the effect of nullifying the apparent consent given by Maureen. According to general principles, it would seem to be that if the deception relates to a *fundamental* matter, then any consent given will be void. Where on the other hand, the deception relates to a *non-fundamental* matter, it is likely to be merely voidable at the option of the victim when she discovers the truth. These principles can be illustrated by reference to the case of *R v Williams* (1923) where a singing teacher told his pupil that she needed an operation to improve her voice. The 'operation' consisted of him having sexual intercourse with her. Not surprisingly, perhaps, the court rejected his defence of consent on the grounds that the victim had been deceived into consenting to something that was *fundamentally* different from that which occurred. If, however, the victim had realised that what was being suggested was sexual intercourse, but had been deceived into believing that a side-effect of this activity would be the improvement of her voice, then there would have been a *non-fundamental* mistake which would not have negated her consent. Applying these principles to Richard's situation, it would seem that the fraudulently induced mistake as to identity would probably be considered to of a non-fundamental nature and, thus, not negate Maureen's consent.

Keith's liability

When Keith punches Richard on the nose he may incur liability in relation to common assault and battery or, if bodily harm has been caused, s 47 of the Offences Against the Person Act 1861. Since both the *actus reus* and *mens rea* requirements of these offences would appear to be satisfied, attention ought to focus on the availability of any relevant defences.

At common law the defence of self-defence would be available to Richard if he was found to have used reasonable force to defend himself from attack.

Obviously, the crucial issue in Keith's case would be whether his use of force was reasonable in the circumstances. On the basis of *R v Williams (Gladstone)* (1984), it would appear that Keith would be entitled to be judged on the facts as he honestly believed them to be, and, therefore, would be permitted to use a degree of force that was reasonable in the context of what he perceived to be happening. Under this principle it was for the jury to decide whether the force used was reasonable in the circumstances as the defendant believed them to be. However, it in *R v Scarlett* (1993), Beldam LJ seems to have extended the *Gladstone Williams* rule by stating that provided the defendant 'believed the circumstances called for the degree of force used, he was not to be convicted even if his belief was unreasonable'. If this is correct, it seems that it is the defendant's rather than the jury's judgment of what is a 'reasonable' degree of force that matters.

If we apply these principles to Keith's situation it appears somewhat doubtful as to whether he will succeed with the defence of self-defence. Obviously, he believes that he is the victim of an unwanted homosexual advance from Richard, but he would surely have difficulty in convincing a court that he honestly believed that the degree of force used was reasonable in these circumstances. After all, Richard has merely inflicted a battery in the sense of the 'least touching of another' and the response of a punch on the nose seems to be out of proportion with the relatively trivial nature of the offence. Moreover, a fundamental although obvious point that should be made is that common law self-defence allows reasonable force to be used for purely defensive purposes, not, as may well have happened in this case, for the purposes of retaliation or the expression of feelings of outrage.

Exactly the same issues would be relevant if Keith raised the common law defence in parallel with the statutory defence contained in s 3(1) of the Criminal Law Act 1967 which provides that:

'A person may use force as is reasonable in the circumstances in the prevention of crime, or in effecting or assisting in the lawful arrest of offenders or suspected offenders or of persons unlawfully at large.'

Again, the use of force to prevent what is no more than a common battery of a relatively trivial nature would probably be found to be unreasonable even on the defendant's view of what the circumstances necessitated.

That Something Extra   6

Once you have mastered the problem-solving procedure, as applied to the above scenarios, you should be able to provide good and even very good answers to a wide-range of problems in criminal law. However, if you aspire to first-class standard you will need to produce that mysterious something extra which distinguishes the excellent from the good. Although examiners are notoriously vague about precisely what it is that makes a first class paper, nevertheless, it seems that three features are consistently cited in this context: the inclusion of intelligent references to relevant learned articles, a willingness to critically evaluate aspects of the law from within the traditional boundaries of legal doctrine and, finally, the ability to go beyond doctrine and examine the sociopolitical conditions and philosophy which shape the law in specific historical contexts.

Using articles

Throughout your study of criminal law you should try to cultivate the habit of reading relevant articles in journals such as: *The Criminal Law Review*, *The Modern Law Review*, *The Quarterly Law Review*, *The Cambridge Law Journal*, *The Oxford Journal of Legal Studies* and *The Journal of Law and Society*. Given the demands of a modern law degree, you will find it impossible to find time to read all the articles which relate to criminal law, let alone those that deal with background and related issues. Rather than attempt any such 'blanket coverage' you should exercise your discretion so as to select those articles which are of direct relevance to the *main topics* on your syllabus. Indeed, it may be helpful to have a copy of the syllabus and/or teaching schedule to hand when perusing the contents pages of the relevant publications. Sometimes, however, the mere title will provide insufficient information for you to be able to make a sensible assessment of whether it is worth investing the one or two hours required to read the article. In these circumstances you should quickly skim the article, paying particular attention to the opening paragraphs, which often provide a clear summary of the issues to be addressed, the headings, sub-headings and conclusion.

Once you have decided that an article is of direct relevance, the next step is to read it as fully and as carefully as possible. Only a thorough and thoughtful reading will enable you to make the most of the articles you select. After all, there is a major difference between *passive* reading, where the author's argument is simply understood and accepted, and *active* reading which involves integrating the new material into your existing body of legal knowledge. By a reflexive process of moving from article to knowledge and knowledge to article you can begin to form the sort of *critical* appreciation of criminal law which is the hallmark of the first class student.

Of course, it should be remembered that this academic appreciation of learned articles should ultimately be reflected in examinations, if the fate of the first class student with the third class degree is to be avoided. The problem here is how to demonstrate quality legal scholarship, accumulated during a year of intensive study, in the artificial and time constrained environment of the examination. Typically, due to the way that most examination papers are structured, you will only be able to spend about 30 minutes on each question and this means that you will be hard pressed to complete the basic problem-solving procedure, let alone provide a detailed discussion of relevant articles. Although, the heightened appreciation of criminal law that you have acquired through an intelligent and reflective reading of articles should automatically improve the quality of your legal reasoning, it is still important to make one or two specific references to articles during the course of each answer.

There is no need for this kind of specific reference to be at all detailed. Indeed, the *central* argument of an article can often be summarised in one or two sentences and not much more than this can reasonably be expected within the confines of the traditional time constrained and problem based examination paper. In order to capture the essence of each article for later use in examinations it is helpful to complete an index card noting, the author's name, title, date, name and volume of the journal and, most importantly, a short summary of the main argument.

Examiners are often especially impressed by candidates who are able to *critically evaluate* an article by comparing and contrasting the author's argument with that put forward in another publication. This shows that not only has the student read and understood at least two relevant articles, but also is able to relate one to the other in an intelligent way. To illustrate the point in relation to Scenario 5, the discussion of the *actus reus* of attempt could have included brief reference to 'Wrong Turnings on the Law of Attempt' (1991) Crim LR 416 by Glanville Williams and 'Proximity in Attempt: Lord Lane's "Midway Course" ' (1991) Crim LR 576 by KLM Smith. Professor Williams argues that the legislature missed an opportunity to broaden the law of attempt by failing to incorporate something akin to the American 'substantial step' test when enacting the Criminal Attempts Act 1981. This view could have then been compared and contrasted with that of KLM Smith who accepts that the law of attempt is unjustifiably narrow, but who argues that the fault lay with the judiciary rather than the legislature since s 1(1) of the Criminal Attempts Act 1981 has the potential to be interpreted in a way that would give the offence much wider scope. It is this kind of playing off of one article against another, always provided, of course, that the issues discussed are directly relevant to the problem under consideration, which has the potential to earn those valuable extra marks that can make all the difference to the classification of degree awarded.

Principles and policies

Criminal law is not simply a set of clearly defined rules that can be mechanically applied to give a definitive answer to any particular problem scenario. On the contrary, as we have continually noted throughout this book, the rules of law are inherently 'open-textured' and capable of being shaped in many different ways. However, this 'shaping' does not occur simply as the result of random determinations by judges, lawyers and other personnel involved in the administration of the criminal justice system. Rather these decision makers draw upon doctrines, principles and policies which function to mediate the application of the rules and which have acquired legitimacy through repeated usage over time. Although, there has been no systematic legislative or judicial recognition of these principles they have become so well established that they can be regarded as a necessary and complementary part of the law itself.

One way in which you can include that 'extra something' in assignments and examinations is by drawing attention to these broader aspects which underpin the operation of the criminal law. However, it should not be supposed that these principles and policies constitute a non-contradictory field of meaning which operates to 'close' the 'open-textured' nature of legal rules. Although particular principles and policies are sometimes promoted as if they were fundamental and incontrovertible, there are often both theoretical and practical arguments that can be raised against them. Policies can and do run counter to principles and principles sometimes conflict with each other. It is the presence of these tensions and contradictions within the very substratum of the law which can provide such a useful critical framework for the analysis of legislative and judicial decisions in the context of specific problem situations.

It is, of course, not possible, or even desirable, within the ambit of this book to attempt to provide even an outline of the complex principles and policies which underlie the operation of the criminal law. Those who wish to develop their understanding of these matters would be well advised to consult Andrew Ashworth's *Principles of Criminal Law* (1991); a book which well repays careful reading and re-reading. All that can be realistically achieved here is to briefly indicate how such considerations can be applied to two particular issues in order to heighten your awareness of this level of legal analysis.

Many problem questions in criminal law are constructed so as to prompt a discussion not only of the actions of the various characters, but also of their failure or omission to act. Indeed, the attentive reader will have noticed that several of the scenarios contained in the previous chapters similarly involve situations which call for a discussion of liability for failing to act. For example, in our discussion of Scenario 1 we considered Roger's liability for failing to prevent the death of Jasper, in relation to Scenario 3 it was argued that Marnah formed the necessary intent for s 18 of the Offences Against the Person Act 1861 by deciding 'not to move the car', while in Scenario 4 Austin's liability for omitting to refill a drip-feed was considered. This concentration on failure to act reflects the ambivalent approach towards liability for omissions to act in English law. After all, it is often claimed that there is a general rule which limits liability to commissions, but also there seems to have been a steady growth in the number of situations where there is a statutory or common law duty to act.

In our consideration of the various 'omission' situations contained in the previous chapters we adopted the traditional position of 'no liability for failure to act' and then constructed arguments as to whether or not the specific facts could be encompassed within one or other of the recognised exceptions where there is a duty to act. However, we could have added 'something extra' to our discussion at this stage by focusing on the issues of principle and policy which inform the existing legal distinction between acts and omissions.

The apparent contradiction between a legal rhetoric which restricts liability to acts of commission and the reality of the legislative and judicial recognition of increasing numbers of 'duty' situations can be explained by drawing attention to a fundamental tension between opposing principles which underpin this area of the law. One principle which provides such a foundation is *individualism*, which argues that although it may be necessary to place citizens under a duty to act in order to maintain a minimalist state (eg the duty to pay taxes) and special private relationships (eg parental and contractual duties), any further extension of liability would constitute an unjustified restriction on personal freedom. This is because individualism places such a high value on personal autonomy that the imposition of a positive duty to act in situations that might occur by chance (eg a duty to effect an 'easy rescue') would be regarded as an interference with the individual's own goals and life plans.

However, the principle of *collectivism* or *social responsibility*, which emphasises the need for individuals to co-operate to achieve *social* goals, stands in direct contrast to the above view. According to this view, human happiness *and the fullest possible development* of the individual are only possible in the context of a community which accepts the need to legally support human interdependence and mutual support.

In many situations, for example, Scenarios 1 and 3, both principles operate to support the existing law, albeit for different reasons. In relation to the first scenario an advocate of individualism could support Roger's liability for causing the death of Jasper by omission on the grounds of parental duty, whereas the collectivist would justify it on the broader ground of a general social duty to take reasonable care of others. However, in relation to the third scenario, Marnah's liability for causing grievous bodily harm to Bronwen is based on the duty to limit the effects of accidental harm which seems to reflect a collectivist rather than an individualist approach. However, even here individualism plays a part for liability is limited to cases where the defendant is 'responsible' for creating a dangerous situation, albeit accidentally. A collectivist would argue that the criminal law ought to include an offence of failing to take reasonable steps to assist another citizen in peril, quite irrespective of who initiated the dangerous situation. According to this perspective the value of preserving the life or safety of the person in danger far outweighs the value that the individualist places on personal autonomy.

An understanding of the differences between the individualist and collectivist positions can provide a useful analytical tool for explaining and critically evaluating judicial decisions. For example, in *R v Speck* (1977) the defendant was convicted for an offence contrary to s 1 of the Indecency with Children Act 1960. An eight year old girl had approached him and placed her hand on his penis. He allowed her hand to remain there for approximately five minutes during which time he had an erection. He appealed on the basis that he had not committed any '... *act* of gross indecency with or towards a child under the age of fourteen ...' as required by the definition of the offence (emphasis added). His conviction was upheld on the basis that failing to remove the girl's hand could amount to an *invitation* to the child to undertake the act. However, this reasoning reflects a somewhat strained use of language; surely an invitation involves words or positive conduct, after all victims do not *invite* the acts inflicted on them by simply failing to stop them. Moreover, an invitation must of necessity *precede* the act invited and this raises the problem of how long had the girl to keep her hand in place before it could be said that there was an invitation to carry on.

A far simpler solution would have been for the court to uphold the conviction by creating a new common law exception to the general principle prohibiting liability for mere inactivity to the effect that adults have a duty to prevent children from making sexual contact with them. This, however, would involve an explicit recognition of collectivist values, apparently something the court was not prepared to do. When analysed in terms of underlying principle the strange argument that an omission to act could amount to an invitation (which the court implied was really an action after all) becomes explicable as an attempt to uphold the conviction of someone the court considered to be morally culpable while at the same time maintaining an individualist position.

So far we have considered how the tension between the broad opposing principles of individualism and collectivism can be used as an analytical tool to enhance the quality of legal reasoning in relation to the issue of liability for failure to act. In the same way, opposing principles derived from *subjectivist* and *objectivist* approaches to criminal law also have the potential to enable us to obtain a theoretical purchase on specific aspects of problem situations.

The subjectivist approach, itself based on liberal individualist values, maintains that criminal liability should only be imposed on those who are sufficiently aware of what they are doing, and of the possible consequences of their actions, that they can be said to have *chosen* to have acted in that fashion. According to this perspective criminal liability should be based on the choices that individuals make in response to their perception of the circumstances they find themselves in. This general orientation gives rise to three subjective principles that are well grounded in traditional legal doctrine; the *mens rea* principle, the 'belief' and the 'correspondence' principles.

According to the *mens rea* principle defendants should only be held criminally liable for the consequences of acts or omissions which they intended or knowingly risked. This, of course, limits the requisite fault element to that of either intention or 'subjective' recklessness and excludes both strict liability and 'objective' recklessness.

The belief principle complements the *mens rea* principle by recognising that the mental elements of intention or recklessness are not formed in an abstract void, but in relation to circumstances as the defendant believe them to be. Thus, while the *mens rea* principle focuses on the defendant's foresight of the possible *consequences* of his behaviour, the belief principle addresses his perception of the *circumstances* in which he decided to act. In short, this principle maintains that the defendant is entitled to be judged *on the basis of the facts as he believed them to be*.

Further support for the *mens rea* principle is provided by the correspondence principle which maintains that the fault element of an offence should always correspond with the conduct element of the same offence. This correspondence between *mens rea* and *actus reus* should occur in terms of both the timing of these elements and in terms of their seriousness. Thus, if an *actus reus* consists of causing serious injury, the requisite *mens rea* should similarly consist of an intention or recklessness as to causing serious injury. An intention to kill would suffice, since the greater includes the lesser, but an intention to cause minor injury ought not, since the lesser cannot include the greater.

Although the subjectivist approach outlined above tends to dominate legal rhetoric, the reality of legal decision making has been far more varied, upholding subjectivist principles on some occasions and abandoning them in favour of objectivist principles and policies on others. Such objectivism rejects the overriding value placed on individual autonomy by the subjectivists and maintains that criminally liability should be imposed if the overall effect is to prevent further social harm. According to this view the individual defendant should be punished, even though he did not intend or was not reckless as to the harm in question, providing this results in a general deterrent effect which prevents further harm to society. Obviously, this broad principle of objectivism, or social defence, supports many sub-principles and policies such as liability for (objective) recklessness and negligence as well as strict liability and vicarious liability.

Having briefly outlined the subjectivist and objectivist positions we are now in a position to illustrate how this knowledge can be used to critically analyse a specific aspect of the law. Nowhere is the tension between these opposing principles more apparent than in relation to the decision in *Caldwell v MPC* (1982). In this case the House of Lords challenged the traditional subjectivist view that criminal liability should be limited to situations where the defendant foresaw the consequences of his actions and extended the concept of recklessness to include those who failed to think about a risk which would have been obvious to a reasonable person. Since many assignments and examination questions involve situations which call for a fairly detailed consideration of *Caldwell* recklessness, as do several of the scenarios contained in the earlier chapters of this book, there are plentiful opportunities to present a critical analysis of the decision.

The significant part of the decision in *Caldwell* can be briefly stated, Lord Diplock held that a person is guilty of causing criminal damage recklessly if:

'... (i) he does an act which in fact creates an obvious risk that property would be destroyed or damaged and (ii) when he does the act he either has not given any thought to the possibility of there being any such risk or has recognised that there was some risk involved and has nonetheless gone on to do it.'

Clearly, the decision appears to cut across the traditional distinction between different forms of liability, based on the defendant's degree of culpability. Orthodox legal theory had developed since Victorian times on the assumption that liability for serious offences should be linked to a subjective *mens rea* of intention, or recklessness where the accused *adverted* to, or was aware of, the risk. Negligence, consisting of *inadvertence* to risk, was considered less blameworthy and, therefore, not appropriate for the most serious offences, with the notable exception of manslaughter.

However, Lord Diplock did not support the decision in *Caldwell* by explicitly objectivist reasoning to the effect that a person who fails to give any thought to an obvious risk is just as *socially dangerous* as the person who realises the risk. On the contrary, he attacked the advertence/inadvertence distinction by arguing that subjective recklessness was unsatisfactory because it excludes the equally culpable state of indifference. Indeed, it can be argued that a person who has the capacity to appreciate a risk of harm that a reasonable person would recognise, but fails to do so, is more culpable than another person who knowingly takes a slight risk of the same harm. It can be argued that this type of inadvertence would amount to a sort of subjective negligence since the defendant *chose* not to consider the risk in question.

There seems to be a growing recognition among academic lawyers, as against the orthodox subjectivist critique of *Caldwell* recklessness, that the above argument appears to stand up well. The traditional emphasis on awareness of risk did, indeed, narrow the ambit of recklessness too far; excluding both acts done in temper and those committed with indifference to an obvious risk. However, the 'revised subjectivist' rationale suffers from the fundamental weakness that *Caldwell*, when coupled with later decisions which give an objective meaning to the phrase 'obvious risk', has the effect of criminalising people who through no fault of their own, are *not capable* of meeting the standard of the reasonable person. Thus, in *Elliot v C* (1983) an educationally subnormal 14 year old girl could be found guilty of criminal damage for setting fire to a shed even though her appreciation of the risk involved could not match that of the reasonable person. Not surprisingly, it seems to be generally accepted among academic lawyers that if *Cunningham* subjective recklessness is too narrow, then *Caldwell* objective recklessness is too broad. There is evidence of a move towards a more just reconciliation of subjectivist and objectivist principles in *R v Reid* (1992) where the House of Lords seemed to indicate that in exceptional cases, involving defendants who were incapable of appreciating a risk through no fault of their own, there ought to be a subjective interpretation of 'obvious risk'.

Obviously, in an examination situation, there will not be time to include a detailed account of how the tension between subjectivism and objectivism informs the decision in *Caldwell*. However, an appreciation of these underlying issues will enable you to have a better understanding of this confusing area of the law. Moreover, if a particular question specifically focuses on offences involving this form of recklessness you can provide that 'something extra' by *briefly* indicating how the decision represents an ultimately unsuccessful attempt to synthesise subjectivist and objectivist principles.

Contextual approaches

There seems to be an emerging consensus among lecturers and examiners that one possible attribute of a first class student is the ability to synthesise a critical 'internal' account, including issues of principle and policy, with an 'external' approach which locates criminal law within its social and political context. However, there are differences of opinion as to how far the student should go in this direction. This problem can be resolved to some extent by tailoring your 'contextual input' to conform to the philosophy informing the particular course in criminal law that you have chosen to study. A review of the syllabus, reading list and, not least, the content of the lectures themselves should provide a good indication of where you stand in this respect. Very broadly there seems to be three different approaches among those courses which claim to be adopting a 'contextual' philosophy.

Closest to the 'black-letter' end of the continuum is the type of course which tends to not only examine traditional legal doctrine, but also to supplement it by contrasting the 'law in books' with the 'law in action'. For example, attention might focus on the way in which provocation functions in relation to cases involving battered women, or on statistics which indicate the extent to which the defence of insanity is actually raised by defendants.

Located somewhat further along the continuum one finds a more critical approach which seeks to expose the contradictions and tensions within traditional legal doctrine. These conflicts and tensions are then related to the specific historical and political conditions which informed them. In this way historical and social analysis is used to demonstrate how the very structure of the criminal law, far from being based on absolute principles of rationality and justice, has been shaped predominately by the rationalist and individualist ideologies of the Enlightenment. Ideologies, which it is so often argued, are no longer appropriate to a modern industrial society at the end of the 20th century.

At the furthest extreme from 'black-letter' law are those attempts to understand law as a social phenomenon making full use of sociological theory and concepts. In this type of course the contributions of the 'classic' sociological theorists such as Durkheim, Weber and Marx will be studied in order to gain theoretical purchase on the process of legal norm creation, adjudication and change. Concepts such as interest, function, role, structure, culture and class will be used to analyse the law rather than legalistic concepts such as rights, duties and powers. Indeed, the central distinguishing concept of positivist law may itself be challenged with attention also being focused on the informal norms that constitute the 'living law' or 'popular justice'.

Of course, it is important to remember that if you are dealing with the kind of problem scenarios considered in the earlier chapters of this book your approach should be *predominately* that of the 'black-letter' lawyer. A fully fledged sociological approach would clearly be inappropriate in relation to the type of syllabus examined by means of these traditional problem questions. However, even the most traditional of examiners will be impressed by the student who can not only apply the problem-solving procedure, but also produce some evidence of an appreciation of the social and political context in which the law is both constructed and applied. A sensible course of action, therefore, would be to limit your 'contextual input' to the first two approaches outlined above.

In order to demonstrate how this can be achieved, some of the issues raised in our earlier discussions will be revisited and given a contextual treatment, albeit a necessarily limited one.

Scenario 1

Although this constitutes a very traditional 'black-letter' problem and should undoubtedly be treated predominately from within that perspective, there is still the opportunity to attempt very briefly to locate the operation of the legal rules within a social context. For example, attention could be drawn to some of the following points.

(1) The scenario involves domestic violence; the attempted murder of a wife by her husband and the actual murder of a son by his father. In this respect the scenario appears fairly realistic for homicide is overwhelmingly domestic and violence within the family not infrequent (Lacey *et al, Reconstructing Criminal Law* (1990) p 218).

(2) Although there is no separate category of 'domestic violence' included in the annual Criminal Statistics it does seem that there is a consistent tendency for killers to be male and victims female (Cameron and Frazer, *The Lust to Kill, Polity* (1987) p 8).

(3) While the homicide rate of those under 12 months is nearly three times that of the population as a whole, children, like Jasper, aged between five and 15 years are much less at risk than either those younger or older. Indeed, the rate for those under five is eight times that of the older child (Walmsley, *Personal Violence* (1986) p 7).

Scenario 4

In relation to this scenario it would be possible to briefly draw attention to the tension between legal and medical conceptions of death. The basic point to be made here is that the courts still seem to favour the cardio-respiratory concept of death whereas 'brain death', or death of the brainstem, is now almost universally accepted by the medical profession as constituting total death (Lamb, 'The Death of Reason in Intensive Care', *Times Higher Educational Supplement*, 25 March 1988, p 17). The judicial approach in cases such as *R v Malcherek* and *Steel* (1981)) together with the refusal of the Criminal Law Revision Committee, in its report on Offences Against the Person (1980), to consider a new legal definition of death, indicates a commitment to a conception of death that has not been generally accepted in the medical profession since the 1950s.

In addition, some of the philosophical issues comprising the 'euthanasia debate' could be mentioned when considering Austin's liability for the death of Julie and Maureen. A distinction could be drawn between *passive* euthanasia where the patient is not killed, but merely allowed to die and *active* euthanasia where the patient is killed, for example, by giving a lethal injection. Julie's death, at least on the basis of the facts contained in the 'sting in the tail', would amount to passive euthanasia whereas Maureen's death would constitute active euthanasia. As we have seen, this distinction between act and omission plays an important part in legal reasoning. It can be argued that because Austin omits to re-fill Julie's drip-feed, he will not incur liability for her subsequent death. Of course, this is provided that he is not in breach of duty, but he may not be, since a doctor would still have a contractual and moral duty to alleviate pain and suffering even if the preservation of life was no longer possible (*R v Adams* (1957)).

However, a critical evaluation of the operation of the law in this context could make the point that the legal emphasis on the act/omission distinction in relation to the behaviour of the accused is misplaced. Surely, the key distinction should be between *voluntary, non-voluntary* and *involuntary* euthanasia. Voluntary euthanasia occurs where the patient requests death, non-voluntary euthanasia occurs where the patient is unable to express a wish in the matter and involuntary euthanasia occurs where the patient says that they do not wish to die, but is nevertheless killed or allowed to die. Clearly, the decision not to refill Julie's drip-feed would amount to non-voluntary euthanasia whereas the administration of the lethal injection to Maureen would constitute voluntary euthanasia.

Since, one of the most fundamental elements of the ideology of common law is respect for the liberty of the individual, involuntary euthanasia will undoubtedly be treated as murder. If a terminally ill patient wants to prolong life as much as possible, even at the cost of great pain, that is the individual's right and the law will protect it. Equally, if the law is to maintain consistency with its ideology of protecting individual autonomy, voluntary euthanasia ought not to be murder. Further support for this position can be gained by reference to utilitarian philosophy which asserts that actions and social policies are morally right if they function to increase the amount of happiness in the world or decrease the amount of misery. Clearly, the policy of killing, at their own request, terminally ill patients who are suffering great pain would decrease the amount of misery in the world and, thus, constitute a morally justifiable course of action.

Notice that the utilitarian argument taken to extremes could justify non-voluntary and involuntary euthanasia as well as voluntary. However, the position stated above does not uncritically accept the utilitarian standpoint, but recognises that the promotion of happiness and the avoidance of pain *are not the only morally important things* and should be qualified by the individual's right of self-autonomy. According to this position, Maureen's death should not constitute murder whereas Julie's most probably both should and would.

Obviously, in an examination you will not have time to make all of the above points, let alone explore them in much detail. Nevertheless, because of its contemporary significance and the underdeveloped state of the relevant case law, this scenario does seem to call for some reference to the above arguments, albeit in outline form.

Do's and Don'ts 7

The last chapter attempted to indicate the route by which you could climb to the dizzy summits of legal scholarship. In this chapter we return to base camp by focusing attention on examples of good and bad practice in the technique of answering problem questions in criminal law. Although some of these points will no doubt seem obvious to you, it should be remembered that a surprising number of students needlessly loose valuable marks in examinations and assignments through lack of attention to these basic issues. Indeed, if students could have the disconcerting experience of momentarily changing places with examiners they would immediately appreciate the deficiencies of *structure, content* and *style* that bedevil a large proportion of examination scripts. Armed with this knowledge they could then resume their role as students, quietly confident of enhancing their own examination performance. Unfortunately, this transformation from student to examiner only occurs to a very small select minority, moreover, it appears to be a transition, like crossing the Rubicon, from which there is no return. It is, therefore, essential in order to maximise your potential as both student and potential employee to pay close attention to the following matters.

Structure

Imagine that you stripped a bicycle down to the smallest possible number of constituent parts – the separated links of the chain, spokes, bearings, nuts and bolts etc – and placed them in a jumbled heap on the floor. An inquisitive passer-by might be able to recognise various elements of a bicycle, but would be unable to ascertain whether all the necessary parts were present, let alone whether they could be assembled into a functioning whole. Unfortunately, many assignments and examination scripts are rather like that. An overworked examiner, rapidly reading through, possibly, hundreds of scripts, might be able to detect some areas of relevance, but a lack of any overall organisation often makes it almost impossible to untangle the various issues and lines of argument. Just as a bicycle is a functional way of organising all its necessary constituent parts, so too is a well structured assignment or examination script a way of assembling legal scholarship so as to directly address the concerns of the question. Not only will a sound structure help make the job of the examiner that much easier, but also it will assist the examinee by allowing attention to focus on one aspect of the problem at a time.

Perhaps, we should commence our consideration of how to structure an answer to a problem-question by indicating one or two definite 'don'ts'. An obvious 'don't', although one that a not insignificant number of students indulge in, is the curious practice of rewriting the question, either verbatim or in their own words. Whether or not this is done in the optimistic belief that the examiner will mistake his own question for its answer remains open to speculation. What is quite clear, however, is that this practice will waste valuable time, not gain any marks and might well further irritate an already tetchy examiner.

Another, rather less obvious, 'don't' concerns the provision of a general introduction at the commencement of an answer. Although the question of whether to write an introduction to an examination answer is a problematic one on which lecturers and examiners can and do disagree, it is suggested that, in the case of problem-questions, an introduction is best avoided. Usually such introductions are worthy attempts at locating the problem under consideration within the broad framework of the criminal law, but however laudable such an objective may be it is not an answer to the question. Most examiners would not award any marks at all for the sort of general information relating to criminal liability, such as the nature and need for *actus reus* and *mens rea*, that is often provided by students in their introductory sentences. Indeed, such generalities maybe perceived not only as a waste of the examiner's valuable time, but also as an indicator of a weak student who is avoiding directly addressing the issues inherent in the problem.

Having identified two false starts, perhaps, it is now appropriate to indicate some positive guidelines for structuring an answer to a problem question.

(1)   Use subheadings

A good approach is to consider each party's liability in turn under relevant sub-headings of the 'Roger's liability' type, similar to those used throughout Chapters 2 to 5 of this book. This practice will help keep both the examiner and the student focused on one aspect of the problem at a time, thus making their respective tasks somewhat more manageable as well as ensuring that the question is directly addressed.

(2)   Write in paragraphs

Under each sub-heading scripts should be further structured into paragraphs, each one developing a separate idea. You should think of these paragraphs as building blocks which enable the rapid construction of a legal argument. Of course, the central idea of each paragraph or block would be determined by the, now familiar, problem-solving procedures outlined in Chapter 1 and demonstrated in Chapters 2 to 5. For example, the foundation blocks of a legal argument would be concerned with the identification of relevant offences, while the next layer would consist of definitional blocks which would, in turn, form the basis for those paragraphs forming the overarching capstone of legal reasoning.

(3)   Write in simple sentences

Each paragraph should be, in turn, made up of short clear sentences consisting of readily understandable words. In the heat of an examination it is all too easy for the student to lose the thread of what may be a good argument in a tangled web of words woven out of lengthy sentences containing complex dependent and sub-dependent clauses, colons, semi-colons and parentheses. An essential communication skill that both law students, and practitioners, need to develop is the ability to express complex technical matters in a clear jargon free manner. Indeed, an astute examiner, or client, might well be suspicious that a complex, jargon ridden style is indicative of an affection of scholarship or professional competence which masks an underlying superficiality. Many of the judgments of Lord Denning, although dealing with complex matters, are models of clear English arranged into short simple sentences that are worthy of emulation in this respect. Like his Lordship, always try to write in a readily comprehensible way, using sentences and words which are as simple as the context permits.

(4)   Use simple words

Although the use of technical terms, some of which will inevitably be Latin, cannot be entirely avoided in legal discourse, their use should be restricted to occasions where they aid rather than detract from the attainment of clarity. Avoid trying to impress the examiner by using pseudo-intellectual language of the 'hegemony of the English judiciary' kind, particularly if the meaning of the words used is not absolutely clear to you. As a general rule it is better to eschew (or should it be 'avoid'?) complex and technical terminology whenever possible and try instead to use language which is as simple and as precise as the context permits.

Although the above comments concerning structuring by the use of subheadings, paragraphs, simple sentences and words, might appear all too obvious, the reader would undoubtedly be surprised by the large number of examination scripts which far from exhibiting a carefully constructed cathedral-like edifice of elegant legal reasoning are more reminiscent of the bombed-out remains of post-war Dresden. Such scripts may well contain some jewels hidden among the rubble, but the lack of any clearly defined structure inevitably renders their discovery by even the most diligent of examiners somewhat problematic.

Content

Once again we will commence our discussion of the appropriate type of content of an assignment or examination question by indicating some things that you should not include. Unfortunately, many examination scripts contain large amounts of irrelevant material of both a factual and legal nature for which few or no marks can be awarded. It is, therefore, very important that you 'don't' waste time and exhaust the examiner's limited patience by including such irrelevancies in your answers. Factual irrelevancy occurs where the student introduces a 'red herring' by suggesting a possibility for which there is *no supporting evidence* in the facts of the scenario. Legal irrelevancy, on the other hand, is where a student considers a point in depth which is *not directly relevant* to the problem under consideration. An example of both types of irrelevancy, taken from Scenario 8, should prove sufficient for you to be able to recognise and, hopefully, avoid this kind of material in your assignments and examination answers.

You will no doubt remember that we were informed that 'Roger believed that Jan had been given a lift to the party whereas in fact she had driven herself.' On the basis of this sentence, surprising though it may seem, some misguided students have been known to speculate about the possibility of Jan's liability for taking a conveyance contrary to s 12 of the Theft Act 1968. This kind of consideration is not prompted by any of the facts provided in the scenario and, thus, constitutes a time-wasting diversion that is almost guaranteed to enrage even the most placid of examiners. All too often the inclusion of 'red-herrings' of this nature is then compounded by the omission to adequately deal with matters that are clearly prompted by the facts of the scenario. It is almost as if the slippery student is desperately trying to avoid directly engaging the relevant issues, of which they are, presumably, unsure, in favour of dragging in matters about which they feel more confident. Such tactics are patently obvious and only function to heighten the critical awareness of the suspicious examiner who would by now be in a state of 'red alert'.

As we have noted, legal, as opposed to factual irrelevancy, occurs when too much detail is provided about legal issues which are *non-problematic* in the context of the problem under consideration. An example of this, also based on Scenario 8, would be an extended discussion of the nature of 'property', in relation to the possible criminal damage to the orange juice, including a restatement of the definition contained in s 10(1) of the Criminal Damage Act 1971 and references, by way of analogy, with s 4 of the Theft Act 1968. Obviously, the orange juice, since it is of a tangible nature, amounts to 'property' within the meaning of the Act and consequently there is little point in saying much more than this. The gratuitous display of rote-learning that is not *directly relevant* to the problematic issues raised by the question will earn few if any marks.

Another all too common tendency to avoid is that of 'skating over' or oversimplifying the issues raised in relation to the facts of the scenario. Some aspects of law involve quite complex principles that can themselves be subject to some confusion and uncertainty, in addition, as we should be only too well aware by this stage, the facts provided are often 'open-textured' and capable of different interpretations. In the face of such complexity and uncertainty it is hardly surprising that, as a psychological defence mechanism, students tend to evade these difficult areas or, alternatively, reduce them to a state of simplicity which simply does not exist. However, it should be remembered that the examiner has focused on these issues precisely because they are difficult so any attempt to skate over them will inevitably result in the loss of valuable marks. The ability to accurately apply a confused and complex area of law to a fact situation capable of alternative interpretations is a characteristic of the successful law student.

A somewhat similar tendency, also to be avoided, is that of advancing just one argument. As we have consistently noted throughout this book, degree level problems in criminal law often involve issues about which perfectly reasonable alternative arguments can be constructed. Yet, so many students seem to suffer from a curious form of 'tunnel vision', in that they seem to readily recognise and develop one argument and ignore other possibilities. Always try to demonstrate an awareness and appreciation of the multi-faceted nature of the problems you are expected to cope with.

Many of the things you should do in relation to the content of your answers are merely the reverse of the above 'don'ts'. However, it is worth briefly restating these in a positive form:

(1)   Directly address the question

Focus exclusively on the factual and legal issues that are clearly prompted by the situation under consideration. In other words, the shape of your answer should be dictated by the sequence of facts contained in the scenario. The application of the problem-solving procedure of *identification, definition* and *legal reasoning* explained in this book should enable your answer to be tightly tailored so as to fit the facts in this way.

(2)   Critically evaluate the reasoning behind legal rules and principles

The importance of avoiding a tendency to 'skate over' or oversimplify complex areas has been emphasised above. One form that this process often takes is that of simply accepting a legal principle at face value and then attempting to apply it to the facts of the problem under consideration in a rather unreflective way. Instead, you should be prepared to critically evaluate the reasoning underlying the relevant principle and then relate that reasoning to the specific facts presented in the scenario. In this way long cherished principles can be, at least sometimes, sensibly challenged rather than just mindlessly applied. It is this sort of reasoning which can make solving problems in criminal law such a creative and exciting activity; where everything, in a sense, is up for grabs. Consider, for example, the following extract from a very common form of contrived fact situation:

> *During a mountaineering holiday in North Wales, Peter, who was roped to Terry, lost his grip and slid over the edge of a sheer drop. Terry, realising that he too would shortly be pulled over the edge by Peter's weight, reluctantly cut the rope. Peter fell to his death on the rocks below.*

Obviously, this scenario has been designed to initiate a discussion concerning the availability of the defence of necessity. Most students would, undoubtedly, state the famous principle, laid down by the House of Lords in *R v Dudley and Stephens* (1884), that necessity is unlikely to ever successfully found a defence to homicide. Some students would then go on to refer to the reasoning behind this decision, as stated by Lord Coleridge CJ, that Christian ethics are based on the idea of self-sacrifice, actually giving up one's own life to save others, and the impossibility of choosing between the value of one person's life and another's. However, relatively few students would make the crucial final step of critically evaluating that reasoning in relation to the facts of the problem. Such an evaluation could make the point that modern Britain is predominately a secular rather than a Christian society and that, in any case, the facts of the problem under consideration do not permit even the possibility of Terry sacrificing himself in order to save Peter. Moreover, the problem of how to select the victim referred to by Lord Coleridge CJ does not apply in these circumstances as Peter has been, in a sense, self-selected by accidentally loosing his grip.

It is this sort of consideration which is required in order to elevate legal study from the tedious and barely satisfactory regurgitation of rote-learning to the higher intellectual domain of critically reflective thought.

(3)   Make correct use of authority

Only cite authorities which refer to legal principles which are of direct relevance to the facts contained in the scenario. Try to briefly and accurately state the *principle* established in a particular case rather than provide a description of the facts. The facts of a case should only be referred to where it is necessary to compare them with those contained in the problem scenario in order to argue whether or not the principle is actually applicable. For example, in relation to the above mountaineering scenario, a mere restatement of the well known facts of *R v Dudley and Stephens* would be unlikely to merit the allocation of any additional marks. However, a reference to those facts for the purpose of drawing a material distinction between them and those of the scenario, in terms of the issue of victim selection, would clearly call for the awarding of more marks.

(4)   State alternative arguments

Throughout this book we have noted both the often ambiguous aspects of fact situations and the 'open-textured' nature of law. Where the facts are uncertain it is not your responsibility to adopt one particular interpretation and exclude others from consideration. On the contrary, your answer should be based on *alternative* constructions of the incomplete or ambiguous facts provided. Similarly, where the law is capable of different interpretations, as is the case more often than not, these alternatives should be stated, evaluated and applied to the particular facts of the problem.

Style

Although the following points are included under the heading of 'style', do not be fooled into thinking that these matters are merely peripheral to the writing of a good assignment or examination answer. In reality structure, content and style all combine to produce an overall impression of the quality of your work in the mind of the examiner. You cannot, therefore, afford to ignore these important matters. Once again we will start by highlighting some stylistic 'don'ts' before going on to note some examples of good practice that you should try to cultivate.

Perhaps an obvious point, although one that is worth emphasising, is the importance of trying to purge your writing of slang expressions and clichés. One examination script, which I had the dubious pleasure of marking, included the memorable phrase, 'If Steve is *done* for murder he will *go down* for life' (Italics added). While this kind of statement is likely to alienate the examiner and reduce the overall quality of the answer, the same ideas, expressed in the more eloquent form of, 'If Steve's liability for murder is established then he will receive the mandatory life sentence' may well achieve an extra mark or two.

Another practice to avoid is that of discussing the liability of the parties in terms of the offences that they may be *charged* with. What charges are likely to be brought in a particular situation depends upon prosecution *policy* and *discretion* as well as the liability of the parties. Since most undergraduate courses in criminal law focus primarily on issues of substantive law rather than prosecution policy and practice, it is inaccurate to couch your answers in terms of *charges* when you should really be considering *liability*. Whilst one hopes that in practice there is a relationship between the two, they clearly are not the same thing.

Our final 'don't' refers to the provision of a bibliographical list of cases, textbooks and articles at the end of an assignment or examination question. Although students often seem to have been encouraged at school to include these lists at the end of essays and projects, they are quite unnecessary in the case of short law assignments or examination questions. Brief references to cases and other published works to which you make explicit reference should be provided at the appropriate place in the text of your answer. There can be little point in providing the titles of standard textbooks and leading cases, let alone including, as some students have been known to do, 'lecture notes' and 'handouts' in a general bibliographical list.

In contrast to the matters mentioned above, you should try to cultivate a style of writing that encompasses the following points:

(1)   Spell correctly

In the past there was a tendency to assume that 'A' level students would automatically emerge from secondary or further education with the ability to spell correctly. Even when confronted with direct evidence to the contrary, law lecturers, in rather an elitist manner, tended to doggedly concentrate on matters of substance and ignore poor spelling as being a mere technical matter that was somehow not worthy of their consideration. However, in recent years pressure for a change of attitude has originated from the closer co-operation between colleges, professional bodies and employers. For example, during a recent conference a training officer from the Law Society informed the delegates that seemingly increasing numbers of law graduates, including those who possessed a very good class of degree, were apparently incapable of writing letters and documents free from spelling mistakes. In his view the institutions of higher education were the 'employer's last defence' against this kind of graduate who could seriously jeopardise the credibility of the law firm by sending mis-spelt communications to clients. The implicit solution was simple; if they can't spell fail them. This view, whilst not universally accepted among law examiners does seem to be gaining ground. After all, there is clearly no justification for course designers to emphasise 'communication skills' that are 'integrated throughout the syllabus' without also accepting that assessment criteria should take account of poor spelling.

Examiners are likely to take a particularly dim view of spelling mistakes appearing in assignments where the student has both time to proof read the work prior to submission and access to dictionaries or spell-check facilities of word-processing programmes. Although perhaps somewhat more lenient in relation to time constrained closed book examinations, examiners are hardly likely to be impressed by poor spelling, particularly the misspelling of legal terms and phrases. Make sure you proof read, check suspect words with either a *dictionary* or *spell-check* facility whenever possible and take the trouble to *learn to spell* legal terms.

(2)   Write neatly

Always aim to write in a neat legible fashion. Obviously, if an examiner cannot read what you have written he will be unable to award you any marks at all. Moreover, if a hard pressed examiner finds it difficult and time consuming to decipher your script he may well abandon the effort. Indeed, if your course is one of the increasing number that emphasises the importance of communication skills, a reduction of marks for barely legible writing would be inevitable.

(3)   Adopt an objective style

Avoid a subjective style of the 'I think that Boris will be liable for theft' kind. Instead try to always phrase your answer in an objective fashion. For example, the above statement could have been presented in the objective form of 'It appears that Boris will be liable for theft'.

(4)   Use quotation marks correctly

Some misguided students have been known to try to create a spurious impression of scholarship by enclosing their own summaries of principles in quotation marks. This practice is self-defeating since it is almost always obvious that the alleged quotation has in fact been concocted by the student. An alternative strategy, particularly prevalent in assignments, and equally obvious to the alert examiner, is that of copying an author's words without any form of acknowledgement at all. It is, of course, plagiarism to present another's words as one's own and in order to avoid this grave academic offence quotation marks should always be inserted at the beginning and end of the quoted material. Whenever this is done the source of the quotation should be cited.

Each year law lecturers and examiners undergo the distressing experience of witnessing able and hard-working students who somehow fail to 'get it together' in formal assessments. Often this under-performance seems to occur not as a result of a lack of substantive knowledge, but because students have little idea of what is expected in terms of the *structure, content* and *style* of assignments and examination scripts. Hopefully, the above information, opinions and advice will function rather like a 'friendly examiner', enabling students to achieve their full potential.

Concise Notes 8

The traditional undergraduate course in criminal law, like the traditional text-book, demands that the student cope with both breadth and depth. Unfortunately, this sheer bulk and complexity sometimes tends to militate against a comprehensive understanding of the subject matter. One purpose of this chapter is to provide a corrective overview of the basic rules and principles of criminal law; a skeletal framework on which students will be able to locate their more detailed learning. The concise notes are also intended to function as a quick revision guide; both to enable a better appreciation of the various problem scenarios contained in earlier chapters and for examination purposes.

Figure 10

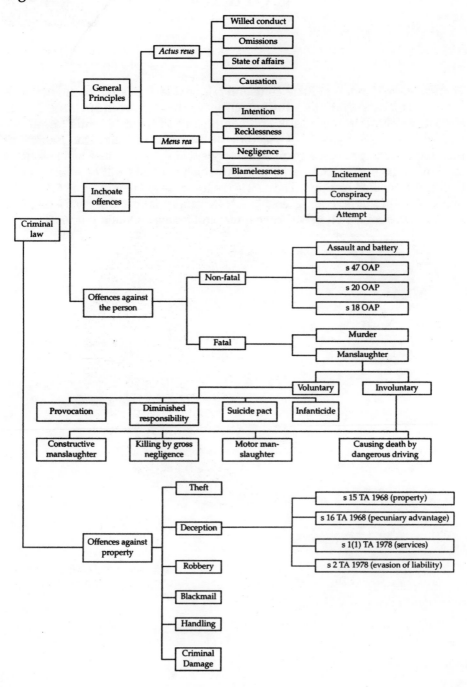

General principles

The nature of a crime

A crime is conduct which has been defined as such by statute or by the common law.

Generally, a person may not be convicted of a crime unless he has acted in a proscribed way (ie the *actus reus*) with a defined state of mind (ie the *mens rea*). The main exception to this are crimes of strict liability where no *mens rea* need be proved.

Figure 11

Crime = *actus reus* + *mens rea* + absence of a valid defence

The prosecution must prove the existence of the *actus reus* and *mens rea* beyond reasonable doubt. This is sometimes referred to as the '*Woolmington* rule' (*Woolmington v DPP* (1935)).

The *actus reus*

Definition

The *actus reus* consists of all the elements in the statutory or common law definition of the offence except the accused's mental element.

An *actus reus* must be proved

An *actus reus* must be proved. If there is no *actus reus* there cannot be a crime. A case which illustrates this principle is *R v Deller* (1952).

The conduct must be willed

It must be proved that the defendant *willed* the action proscribed in the *actus reus*. If the defendant's muscles acted without the control of his mind then he will be able to plead automatism (see *per* Lord Denning in *Bratty v Attorney General for Northern Ireland* (1963)). However, the plea of automatism will fail if the defendant is at fault in bringing about the autonomic state (unless the crime is one of 'specific intent'). Cases which illustrate this point are *R v Lipman* (1970) and *R v Bailey* (1983).

The plea of automatism will not be available where the cause of the behaviour in question is a 'disease of the mind' or, indeed, a disease of the body that affects the mind (*R v Sullivan* (1984)). In these circumstances the relevant defence will be that of insanity rather than automatism.

A state of affairs as an *actus reus*

Exceptionally, the *actus reus* of an offence may not require any willed action at all; it may be enough if a specified state of affairs is proved to exist. Two frequently cited cases involving this type of offence are *R v Larsonneur* (1933) and *Winzar v Chief Constable of Kent* (1983).

Omissions

As a general rule, a person is not criminally liable for what they do not do. However, there are exceptions where the defendant is under a positive duty to act:

(1) duty arising from statute (eg the duty under the Road Traffic Acts to report accidents involving injury);

(2) duty arising from a family relationship (*R v Gibbens and Proctor* (1918); R v *Instan* (1893));

(3) duty arising from contract (*R v Pittwood* (1902));

(4) duty to limit the harm caused by the defendant's accidental acts (*R v Miller* (1983));

(5) duty owed where an *undertaking* has been given and there is *reliance* on that undertaking (*R v Stone and Dobinson* (1977)).

Causation

If the *actus reus* requires the occurrence of certain consequences it is necessary to prove that the defendant caused those consequences.

Firstly it must be established that the defendant's actions were a cause *in fact* of the prohibited consequence. This can be achieved by posing the question 'but for what the defendant did would the consequence have occurred?' If the answer is 'no' then the defendant's act was a cause in fact of the consequence. The case of *R v White* (1910) provides an illustration of a situation where the prosecution were unable to establish causation in fact. White had placed cyanide in his mother's drink, but the medical evidence indicated that she died of heart failure before the poison could take effect. In these circumstances the question 'would she have died but for what he did?' would be answered in the affirmative, she would have died anyway, thus disproving causation.

However, not all instances of causation in fact will render a defendant liable because some acts will be too remote a cause or too minimal; it is, therefore, also necessary to establish causation *in law*. One way in which the courts have approached this issue is to consider whether the defendant's action was 'an operative and substantial cause' (*R v Smith* (1959)). Accordingly, only if the defendant's act constituted the setting in which some other cause operated would the courts be likely to find that the chain of causation was broken.

An alternative approach to causation in law that the courts often adopt is simply to consider whether or not the consequence in question was *reasonably foreseeable*.

However, a defendant's action would still constitute a cause in law, even though the particular consequence in question was not reasonably foreseeable. This could occur in three ways:
(1) if the victim suffered from a physical or mental condition which rendered him especially vulnerable (*R v Blaue* (1975));
(2) if the victim neglected an injury caused by the defendant (*R v Holland* (1841));
(3) if the victim received negligent medical treatment (*R v Smith* (1959)).

It appears that *gross* medical negligence would break the chain of causation (*R v Jordan* (1956)).

Finally, note that a failure to establish causation may result in the defendant being liable for attempting the crime in question.

These rules relating to causation have been summarised in the following flow chart.

Figure 12

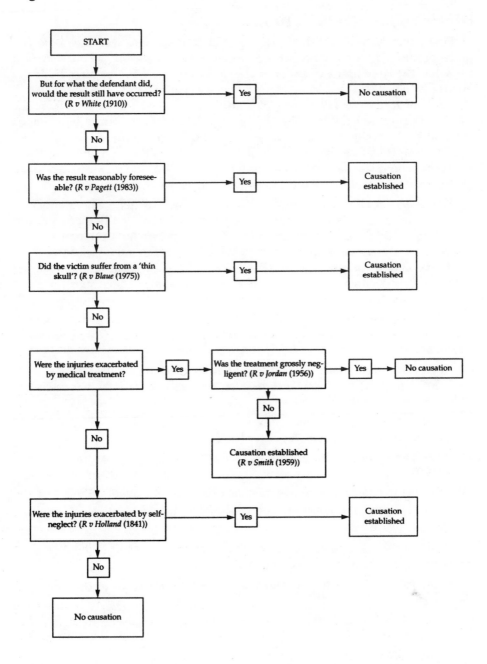

The *mens rea*

Definition

The term *mens rea* refers to the mental element in the definition of the crime.

Intention

There are two types of intention: *direct* and *indirect*. Direct intention consists of foreseeing and desiring the consequence of one's conduct (ie a result is intended when it is the actor's purpose). A jury may infer that a result is indirectly intended even though it is not desired, when:

(1) the result is a *virtually certain* consequence of the act; and

(2) the actor knows that it is a virtually certain consequence (*R v Hancock and Shankland* (1986); *R v Nedrick* (1986)).

Recklessness

Recklessness is the taking of an unjustifiable risk. There are two types:

(1) the conscious taking of an unjustified risk (*R v Cunningham* (1957)); and

(2) the conscious or unconscious taking of an obvious risk (*MPC v Caldwell* (1982)).

Negligence

A negligent action is one that is unreasonable in the circumstances. Gross negligence consists of a major deviation from the standard of reasonable behaviour.

Blamelessness

A person is blameless if they have acted reasonably in the circumstances. However, even 'blameless' behaviour can attract criminal sanctions in the case of crimes of *strict liability*.

Transferred malice

If the defendant, with the *mens rea* of a particular crime, does an act which causes the *actus reus* of the same crime, he is guilty, even though the result, in some respects is an unintended one (*R v Latimer* (1886)).

However, if the defendant, with the *mens rea* of a particular crime, does an act which causes the *actus reus* of *another crime*, he will not be liable under the doctrine of transferred malice (*R v Pembliton* (1874)).

Coincidence of *actus reus* and *mens rea*

The *mens rea* must coincide at some point in time with the act which causes the *actus reus* (*R v Jakeman* (1983)). However, the courts are sometimes prepared to hold that the *actus reus* consisted of a *continuing act* and that the defendant is liable if he formed the requisite *mens rea* at some point during this continuing act (*R v Thabo Meli* (1954); *R v Church* (1966); *R v Le Brun* (1992)).

Ignorance or mistake of law

Ignorance of the *criminal* law is no defence, but a mistake of *civil* law maybe a defence, provided it negates the *mens rea* for the offence in question (*R v Esop* (1836); *R v Smith* (1974)).

Inchoate offences

Incitement

Definition

An incitement is an attempt to influence the mind of another to the commission of a crime.

Actus reus

The central conduct of the offence can take various forms: *suggestion, proposal, request, encouragement, persuasion, threats* or *pressure* (*Race Relations Board v Applin* (1973)).

The incitement must reach the mind of the incitee (*R v Banks* (1873)). Where the incitement does not reach the mind of the incitee there is an *attempted* incitement (*R v Ransford* (1874)).

Since the act incited must be one which would be a crime by the *person* incited, the incitee must know of the facts that make the conduct incited criminal (*R v Curr* (1968)).

At common law the offence of inciting incitement exists (*R v Sirat* (1986)). However, s 5(7) of the Criminal Law Act 1977 abolished the offence of inciting conspiracy. Therefore, it seems that a common law offence of inciting incitement will now only exist where the incitement is based on threats or pressure (*R v Evans* (1986)).

Mens rea

There are three constituent elements of the *mens rea* of incitement:

(1) an intention to incite (*Invicta Plastics v Clare* (1976));

(2) an intention that the incitee act on the incitement (*Invicta Plastics v Clare* (1976));

(3) knowledge or belief that the incitee knows that what is being incited is unlawful (*R v Curr* (1968)).

If the defendant believes that the incitee lacks the *mens rea* for the crime in question then he intends to commit the crime through an innocent agent and may be guilty as the principal or an abettor, but is not guilty of incitement.

Soliciting murder

It is a statutory offence contrary to s 4 of the Offences Against the Person Act 1861 (as amended) to:

'... solicit, encourage, persuade or endeavour to persuade or ... propose to any person, to murder any other person.'

The principles relating to common law incitement would seem to also apply to this offence.

Statutory conspiracy

Definition

By s 1(1) of the Criminal Law Act 1977, as amended by s 5 of the Criminal Attempts Act 1981:

'... if a person agrees with any other person or persons that a course of conduct shall be pursued which, if the agreement is carried out in accordance with their intentions, either:

(a) will necessarily amount to or involve the commission of any offence or offences by one or more of the parties to the agreement; or

(b) would do so but for the existence of facts which render the commission of the offence or any of the offences impossible,

he is guilty of conspiracy to commit the offence or offences in question.'

Actus reus

The *actus reus* of a statutory conspiracy consists of an *agreement* on a 'course of conduct' that will 'necessarily' involve the commission of an offence etc.

Merely talking about the *possibility* of committing an offence is not sufficient (*R v O'Brien* (1974)).

It is not necessary for every party to a conspiracy to be aware of the existence of every other party. The agreement can take the form of a *chain*, where A agrees with B who then agrees with C and so on, a *wheel*, where numerous parties agree on the same course of conduct with a central figure, or a *cluster*, where several parties simultaneously agree.

Figure 13

Chain

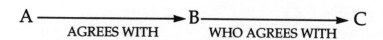

Wheel

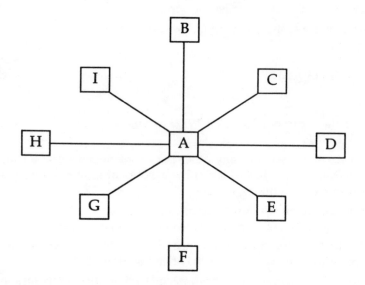

Cluster

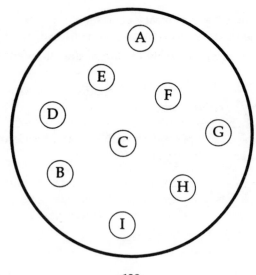

Section 2 of the Criminal Law Act 1977 provides that *victims, spouses* and *children under 10 years old* cannot be parties to a conspiracy.

If the words '... necessarily amount to ... the commission of any offence ...' were construed strictly it would be impossible to secure any convictions for conspiracy. This is because the prosecution would be unable to prove beyond reasonable doubt that the defendant's plan would *necessarily* have resulted in the commission of an offence. Thus, 'course of conduct' must be interpreted to include the defendant's intended consequences (*R v Reed* (1982)).

Mens rea

The defendant must intend to agree on the commission of a particular offence and intend that the offence should be committed.

Intention is required even where the offence agreed upon is capable of being committed with a lesser degree of *mens rea* (*R v Siracusa* (1989)).

According to some interpretations of Lord Bridge's speech in *R v Anderson* (1986) it is not necessary to prove that the defendant intended that the offence be committed, but it must be proved that there was an intention to *play some part* in the carrying out of the agreement. However, the courts have tended to clarify, or reinterpret Anderson in both these respects. It would now appear that a conspirator can 'play a part' simply by agreeing that others should commit the offence (*R v Edwards* (1991), *R v Siracusa* (1989)).

It appears that there is no such offence as a statutory conspiracy to do acts of secondary participation, although there is an offence of common law conspiracy to aid and abet (*R v Hollinshead* (1985); R *v Po Koon-tai* (1980)).

Impossibility is no defence to conspiracy (s 5 Criminal Attempts Act 1981) ie the defendants are judged according to the facts as they believed them to be.

Common law conspiracy

Section 5(2) and (3) of the Criminal Law Act 1977 preserves two forms of common law conspiracy: conspiracy to *defraud* and conspiracy to *corrupt public morals and outrage public decency.*

Conspiracy to defraud

A conspiracy to defraud was defined in *Scott v MPC* (1975) as an agreement to dishonestly deprive a person of something or to interfere in that person's proprietary rights. However, following the decision of the Privy Council in *Wai Yu-Tsang v R* (1991) all that may be required for a common law conspiracy to defraud is proof that '... the conspirators have dishonestly agreed to bring about a state of affairs which they realise will or may deceive the victim ...'. It would, therefore, seem that conspiracies to defraud are not limited to cases of intention to cause economic loss to the intended victim.

The *mens rea* for conspiracy to defraud consists of an intention to defraud and dishonesty. Lord Goff, in *Wai Yu-Tsang v R* (1991) defined an intention to defraud as simply '... an intention to practice a fraud on another, or an intention to act to the prejudice of another man's right'.

Where dishonesty is in issue, the test laid down in *R v Ghosh* (1982) would be applied.

Conspiracy to corrupt public morals or outrage public decency

A conspiracy to corrupt public morals is an agreement that if carried out would be likely to involve conduct '... which a jury might find to be destructive of the very fabric of society' (*per* Lord Simon in *Shaw v DPP* (1962)).

A conspiracy to outrage public decency is an agreement which if carried out would be likely to disgust and annoy members of the public.

There is some uncertainty as to whether or not there is a substantive offence of corrupting public morals (*Shaw v DPP* (1962)), although it now seems clear that there is a substantive offence of outraging public decency (*Knuller v DPP* (1973); *R v Gibson and Another* (1991)).

Attempt

Definition

By s 1(1) of the Criminal Attempts Act 1981:

'If with intent to commit an offence to which this section applies, a person does an act which is more than merely preparatory to the commission of the offence, he is guilty of attempting to commit the offence.'

Actus reus

It must be proved that the defendant has gone beyond mere preparation although it is not necessary for the 'last act' prior to the commission of the offence to have occurred (*R v Gullefer* (1990)).

Mens rea

The defendant must have the *intention* to commit the offence in question. Following the decision in *R v Walker and Hayles* (1990) it appears that indirect intent will suffice.

Where an offence requires *mens rea* as to a circumstance, such as recklessness as to whether the victim of rape consents to intercourse, then the prosecution will have to prove *intention* as to the central conduct (ie intercourse) and reckless-ness (of the *Cunningham* type) as to consent.

Impossibility is no defence (*R v Shivpuri* (1985)). The defendant is judged on the facts as he believed them to be.

Participation

Introduction

Cases involving more than one defendant in the commission of an offence are commonplace. The law divides these parties into two categories:

(1) principals – those whose conduct constitutes the *actus reus* of the offence in question; and

(2) accomplices – those who help in some way.

It is possible to have *joint principals*, for example, where two people stab a victim, and to be a principal *via* the doctrine of *innocent agency*.

Definition

Section 8 of the Accessories and Abettors Act 1861 provides:

> 'Whosoever shall aid, abet counsel, or procure the commission ... (of an offence) ... shall be liable to be tried, indicted, and punished as a principal offender.'

Actus reus

The *actus reus* required for liability as an accomplice consists of one of the following forms of conduct:

(1) *aiding* – helping;

(2) *abetting* – encouraging at the time of the offence. Note that mere presence at the scene of the crime will not suffice to constitute encouragement (*R v Clarkson* (1971));

(3) *counselling* – advising, encouraging, persuading, instructing, pressuring or threatening before the offence;

(4) *procuring* – causing (*Attorney General's Reference No 1 of 1975* (1975)).

Mens rea

The requisite *mens rea* for liability as an accomplice consists of two elements: an *intention* to assist in the commission of the offence and *knowledge* of the type of crime intended (*R v Bainbridge* (1960)).

In relation to murder it must be proved that the accomplice foresaw that death or grievous bodily harm was a *possible* incident of the planned offence being carried out (*R v Hyde* (1991)). This rule applies even where the defendant encourages or assists *before* the commission of the offence, knowing that there is a real or substantial risk that the principal offender will kill or cause grievous bodily harm with intent in the course of it (*R v Rook* (1993)).

If the defendant is under a *legal duty* (eg a contractual duty) to aid the principal, for example, by returning property that the principal owns, he will not be liable as an accomplice even though he knows the type of offence that the principal intends to commit (*R v Lomas* (1913)).

Departure from the common design

An accomplice will be liable for all the *accidental*, or unforeseen consequences that flow from the common design being carried out (*R v Baldessare* (1930)).

However, where the principal deliberately departs from the common design, an accomplice ceases to be a party to his actions (*Davies v DPP* (1954)).

Withdrawal

An accomplice can negate liability by withdrawing from the common design, but the withdrawal must be *effective* in the circumstances (*R v Becerra* (1975)).

A withdrawal cannot be effective unless that withdrawal has been effectively communicated to the other parties before the commission of the offence (*R v Rook* (1993)).

Non-fatal offences against the person

Assault and battery

Actus reus

The *actus reus* of an assault consists of *causing the victim to apprehend immediate physical violence* (*Logden v DPP* (1976)).

It is not clear whether words alone can constitute an assault (*R v Meade and Belt* (1823); *R v Wilson* (1955)). However, it seems settled that words can negate an assault (*Tuberville v Savage* (1669)).

The *actus reus* of a battery consists of the least unauthorised touching of another (*Cole v Turner* (1705)).

Mens rea

The *mens rea* for both assault and battery consists of *intention* or *recklessness* of the *Cunningham* variety.

Following the decision of the divisional court in *DPP v Little* (1991) assault and battery are to be charged as statutory offences under s 39 of the Criminal Justice Act 1988.

Offences Against The Person Act 1861: s 47

Definition

Section 47 of the Offences Against the Person Act 1861 provides that it is an offence to commit:

'... any assault occasioning actual bodily harm ...'.

Actus reus

An 'assault' within the meaning of s 47 can consist of either an *assault*, in the technical sense of causing someone to fear immediate unlawful violence, or a *battery* (ie inflicting immediate unlawful violence).

'Occasioning' means the same as 'causing', therefore, the rules described above relating to causation will be relevant. It will be remembered that the main test for establishing causation in law is to ask *whether the result was the reasonably foreseeable consequence of what the defendant was doing*.

In *R v Roberts* (1971), Stephenson LJ said that only if the actions of the victim could be shown to be 'daft' would the chain of causation be broken. However, it is sometimes argued that this *dictum* conflicts with the 'thin skull rule' that the defendant must take his victim as he finds him.

Actual bodily harm was defined in *R v Miller* (1954) so as to include *any hurt or injury likely to interfere with the health or comfort of the victim*. The concept includes 'psychiatric injury' but does not include mere emotions such as fear, distress or panic (*R v Chan-Fook* (1993)).

Mens rea

The *mens rea* is *intention* or *recklessness* of the *Cunningham* type. Either of these two mental states need to be established only in relation to the *initial assault*; it is unnecessary to prove that the defendant intended or foresaw the risk of harm, however slight (*R v Savage* (1991)).

Offences Against The Person Act 1861: s 20

Definition

Section 20 of the Offences Against the Person Act 1861 creates the two offences of:

'... malicious wounding ...' and '... maliciously inflicting grievous bodily harm ...'.

Actus reus

A wounding requires a complete break of all the layers of the victim's skin (*JCC v Eisenhower* (1984)). Grievous bodily harm means *serious harm* (*R v Saunders* (1985)).

In *R v Wilson* (1983) it was decided that 'inflicting' does not necessarily imply an assault. It would appear, therefore, that 'inflicting' simply implies causation.

Mens rea

The word 'malicious' implies a *mens rea* of *intention* or *recklessness* of the *Cunningham* type.

The decision of the court in *R v Mowatt* (1968) placed a 'gloss' on the *Cunningham* definition of recklessness in relation to s 20 in that the defendant is required to have consciously taken an unjustified risk of *some physical harm* (not necessarily amounting to a wound or grievous bodily harm).

Foresight that the victim will be frightened is not enough (*R v Sullivan* (1981)), as stated above, the defendant must have foreseen some physical harm, albeit of only a minor character.

Offences Against The Person Act 1861: s 18

Definition

By s 18 of the Offences Against the Person Act 1861 it is an offence to:

' ... maliciously ... wound or cause any grievous bodily harm ...'.

Actus reus

The *actus reus* consists of either a wound or grievous bodily harm and these terms have the same meaning as they do in relation to s 20, above.

Mens rea

A specific intent to cause grievous bodily harm is required for this offence (*R v Belfon* (1976)).

Which non-fatal offence?

The issue of which non-fatal offence is the most appropriate in any given situation will depend partly on the degree of harm caused and partly on the *mens rea* of the accused. However, as we have seen, examiners often set questions where the facts are 'open' in relation to one or possibly both of these matters. The following flow chart has been designed in order to help you think your way through the above rules and establish which non-fatal offence is the most appropriate in relation to specific situations.

Figure 14

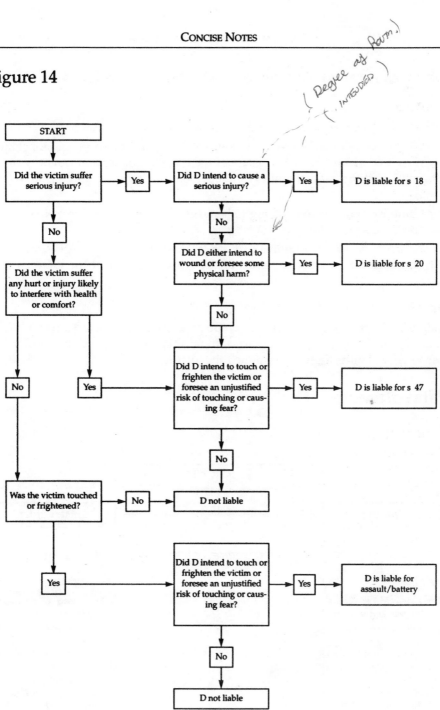

Offences Against The Person Act 1861: s 23 and s 24

Actus reus

Both s 23 and s 24 require the administration of a noxious substance.

Whether or not a substance is noxious will depend upon the circumstances in which it is taken. Such circumstances include the quality and quantity of the substance, and the characteristics of the person to whom it is given (*R v Marcus* (1981)).

'Administering' means causing to be taken, for example, by spraying CS gas into someone's face (*R v Gillard* (1988)).

The *actus reus* of s 23 requires that life must be endangered or grievous bodily harm inflicted as a consequence of the administration of the noxious substance.

Mens rea

Both offences require that the noxious substance be administered *intentionally* or *recklessly* (ie *Cunningham* recklessness), in addition s 24 requires proof of a further intent to injure, aggrieve or annoy the victim.

Fatal offences

Figure 15

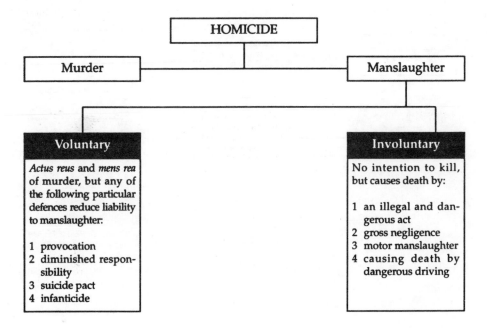

Murder

Actus reus

The *actus reus* of murder is causing the death of a human being within a year and a day (*R v Dyson* (1908)).

A patient kept alive on a life support machine is not regarded as legally dead and is, therefore, capable of being murdered. The original attacker will be held to have caused the death if the machine is turned off as a result of a medical decision made in good faith (*R v Malcherek and Steel* (1981)).

The law of homicide protects the new born child once it becomes capable of independent existence from the mother.

Mens rea

The jury must consider the evidence of what the defendant actually foresaw, and the more evidence there is that the defendant foresaw death or grievous bodily harm, then the stronger the inference that he intended to kill (*R v Hancock and Shankland* (1986)).

In the case of *R v Nedrick* (1986), the House of Lords supplemented the decision in *Hancock* (above) by suggesting that the jury must be satisfied that the defendant foresaw death or grievous bodily harm as a *virtual certainty* before they could infer intention.

Voluntary manslaughter

There are four particular defences that operate to reduce a charge of murder to that of manslaughter: *provocation, diminished responsibility, suicide pact* and *infanticide*.

Provocation

Definition

Section 3 of the Homicide Act 1957 provides:

> 'Where on a charge of murder there is evidence on which the jury can find that the person charged was provoked (whether by things done or by things said or by both together) to lose his self-control, the question whether the provocation was enough to make a reasonable man do as he did shall be left to be determined by the jury; and in determining that question the jury shall take into account everything both done and said according to the effect which, in their opinion, it would have on a reasonable man.'

It follows that anything which, as Devlin J said in *R v Duffy* (1949), causes a '... *sudden and temporary loss of self-control* ...' is capable of amounting to provocation.

The test for provocation.

In order for provocation to succeed the jury must decide that:

(1) the defendant *actually lost his self-control*; and

(2) that a *reasonable person*, sharing the same characteristics as the accused, would have lost his self-control in the same circumstances.

The reasonable person

The case of *Camplin* (1978) is authority for the proposition that the reasonable person should be attributed with the characteristics of the accused in so far as they are relevant to the provoking words or conduct.

In *R v Newell* (1980) it was held that a characteristic must be not only *relevant* to the provocation, but also something *sufficiently permanent*. Thus, intoxication, as distinct from chronic alcoholism, cannot be considered as a characteristic.

Diminished responsibility

Definition

Section 2(1) of the Homicide Act 1957 provides:

'Where a person kills or is a party to the killing of another, he shall not be convicted of murder if he was suffering from such abnormality of mind (whether arising from a condition of arrested or retarded development of mind or any inherent causes or induced by disease or injury) as substantially impaired his mental responsibility for his acts and omissions in doing or being a party to the killing.'

In *R v Byrne* (1960), Lord Parker CJ defined *abnormality of mind* as ' ... as a state of mind that the reasonable person would find abnormal ...'.

Diminished responsibility and intoxication

Where the jury has to deal with both diminished responsibility and intoxication, they should first consider whether the defendant would have killed as he did even if he had not been intoxicated. If the answer is yes, then, they should go on to consider whether he would have been suffering from diminished responsibility when he did so (*R v Atkinson* (1985)).

However, where it is alleged that the defendant was suffering from diminished responsibility caused by the *disease* of alcoholism (as opposed to mere intoxication) the jury must try to establish whether the first drink was taken voluntarily – if so the defence will fail (*R v Tandy* (1989), *R v Egan* (1992)).

Suicide pact

Section 4 of the Homicide Act 1954 contains the defence of suicide pact ie any killing in pursuance of a suicide pact will be treated as manslaughter rather than murder.

Infanticide

Section 1(1) of the Infanticide Act 1938 provides that where a woman kills her child before it reaches the age of 12 months, and there is evidence to show that at the time of the killing the balance of her mind was disturbed by the effect of giving birth, then the jury is entitled to find her guilty of infanticide rather than murder.

Involuntary manslaughter

Constructive manslaughter

Definition

This offence requires proof that the defendant *intentionally* committed a *dangerous criminal act* which resulted in the death of the victim within a year and a day.

Actus reus

The definition of dangerousness as stated in *R v Church* (1966) is as follows:

'... the unlawful act must be such as all sober and reasonable people would inevitably recognise must subject the other person to, at least, the risk of some harm ...'.

In *R v Dawson* (1985) it was held that the jury must be directed to consider the possibility of *physical harm* as opposed to mere emotional disturbance.

Moreover, the reasonable person should be endowed with all the knowledge that the defendant has gained during the course of the crime (*R v Watson* (1989)).

It has been held that the so called 'aimed at doctrine' laid down in *R v Dalby* (1982) should not be construed as requiring proof of an *intention* to harm the victim (*R v Goodfellow* (1986)). Therefore, any act which is both *dangerous* and *criminal* will be capable of forming the *actus reus* of the offence.

Mens rea

All that is required for the *mens rea* is an *intention* to an act which is objectively criminal and dangerous; it is not necessary for the defendant to know that the act is criminal or dangerous (*DPP v Newbury and Jones* (1976)).

Killing by gross negligence

Following the decision of the Court of Appeal in *R v Prentice and Others* (1993) to establish this form of manslaughter the prosecution must prove:

(1) a duty of care;

(2) breach of that duty; and

(3) gross negligence.

Duty of care

It is suggested that this concept, obviously borrowed from the law of tort, is likely to prove unproblematic in the context of the criminal law. Surely there is a general duty to take care not to engage in anti-social behaviour?

Breach of duty

It seems the above duty not to behave in an anti-social way will be breached whenever there is a reasonably foreseeable risk of *injury to health* (as opposed to the risk of *physical injury* required for motor manslaughter – see below) occurring (*R v Stone and Dobinson* (1977)).

Gross negligence

According to the court in *R v Prentice and Others* (above) any of the following states of mind could lead a jury to make a finding of gross negligence:

'(a) Indifference to an obvious risk of injury to health.

(b) Actual foresight of the risk coupled with the determination nevertheless to run it.

(c) An appreciation of the risk coupled with an intention to avoid it but also coupled with such a high degree of negligence in the attempted avoidance as the jury considers justifies conviction.

(d) Inattention or failure to advert to a serious risk which goes beyond 'mere inadvertence' in respect of an obvious and important matter which the defendant's duty demanded he should address.'

Two of these four types of gross negligence, (a) (surely you can only be indifferent to a result which is foreseen?) and (b) are subjective mental states, whereas (c) and (d) are objective. However, each case it seems is subject to the overriding judgment of the jury, '... gross negligence which the jury consider justifies criminal conviction...'

Motor manslaughter

Definition

This common law offence consists of *causing death by reckless driving*.

Actus reus

The defendant must have been driving in such a manner as to cause the death of another road user.

Mens rea

Caldwell recklessness, as modified by the House of Lords in *R v Reid* (1992), is required for this offence. The defendant must have either:

(1) recognised that there was some risk of causing *physical injury* to another road user, but nevertheless went on to take it; or

(2) did not address his mind to the possibility of there being any such *obvious* risk.

The so called 'lacuna', or gap, in *Caldwell* recklessness occurs where the defendant does consider whether there is a risk and decides that there is none. If this mistaken decision is one that a reasonably competent driver would not have made, then the defendant is not liable for motor manslaughter, but may be liable for causing death by dangerous driving.

Causing death by dangerous driving

Causing death by dangerous driving, as defined in s 1 and 2A of the Road Traffic Act 1988, as amended, is, in effect, causing death by grossly negligent driving.

The defendant's driving must fall *far below* the standard of the reasonably competent driver.

It must be obvious to the careful and competent driver that driving in the way that the defendant was actually driving would cause danger of *injury to the person or serious damage to property*.

The following flow chart, which excludes the above driving offences, has been designed to help you decide which is the most appropriate homicide offence.

331
333   324

Figure 16

(WANTED IS THE SAME
  AS INTENDED)

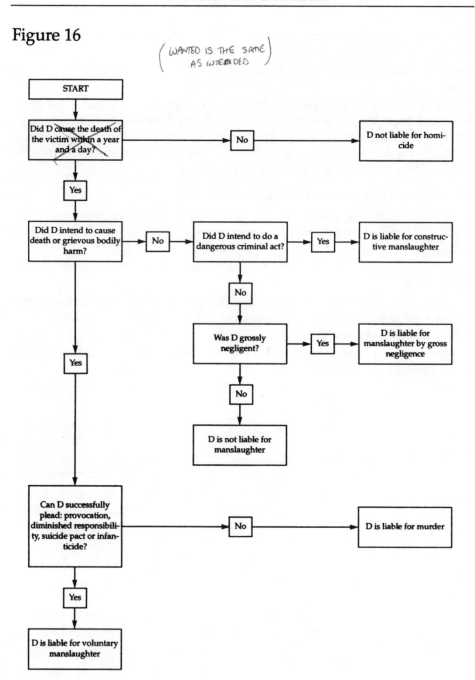

Offences against property

Criminal damage

Offence definitions

There are three offences contained in s 1 of the Criminal Damage Act 1971:

(1) s 1(1) creates the offence of intentionally or recklessly damaging or destroying property belonging to another;

(2) s 1(2) creates the offence of damaging or destroying property with either intention to endanger life, or recklessness as to whether life is endangered.

(3) s 1(3) provides that where property is damaged or destroyed by fire, the offence is charged as arson.

Actus reus

Section 1(1)

'Property' is defined in s 10(1) as anything of '... a tangible nature, whether real or personal, including money ...'.

Section 10(2) provides that property will be treated as 'belonging to another' if that other has custody or control of it or has any proprietary right or interest in it or has a charge on it.

The relevant case law indicated that virtually any *physical interference* with property can amount to 'damage' for the purposes of the Act:

(1) in *Roe v Kingerlee* (1986) it was held that the application of mud to the walls of a cell could amount to damage;

(2) in *Samuel v Stubbs* (1972) a policeman's helmet which had been jumped upon causing a 'temporary functional derangement' was held to be damaged;

(3) in *Hardman and Others v The Chief Constable of Avon and Somerset Constabulary* (1986) the spraying of human silhouettes by CND supporters on pavements was held to constitute damage notwithstanding that the figures would be washed away by the next rainfall.

Mens rea

Section 1(1)

The *mens rea* required for the basic criminal damage offence is an intention to do an act which would cause damage to property belonging to another or being *reckless* (in the *Caldwell* sense) in relation to such an act.

Section 1(2)

The *mens rea* for this 'aggravated' offence of criminal damage is an *intention to endanger life*, or *recklessness* (in the *Caldwell* sense) as to whether this occurs.

Note that the defendant's *mens rea* as to whether life is endangered must extend to the consequences of the criminal damage, and not be limited merely to the act causing the damage (*R v Steer* (1988)).

Defences

Section 5 of the Criminal Damage Act 1971 provides two particular defences to a charge of criminal damage.

Belief in owner's consent

Section 5(2)(a) provides that the defendant has a defence if:

'... he believed that the person or persons whom he believed to be entitled to consent to the destruction of or damage to the property in question has so consented, or would have so consented to it if he or they had known of the destruction or damage and its circumstances.'

It does not matter if the defendant's belief is unreasonable provided it is honestly held.

Defence of property

Under s 5(2)(b) the defendant has a lawful excuse if, in order to protect property, he damaged other property provided he believed:

(1) that the property was in *immediate* need of protection; and

(2) that the means of protection were *reasonable* in the circumstances.

Note that s 5(3) provides that the defendant's belief that his actions are reasonable does not itself have to be reasonable. The defendant is judged on the basis of what *he* considered to be a reasonable course of action in the circumstances.

Theft

Definition

Section 1(1) Theft Act 1968:

' ... dishonestly appropriates property belonging to another with the intention of permanently depriving the other of it ...'.

Actus reus

Property

Section 4(1) defines 'property' as:

'... money and all other property, real or personal, including things in action and other intangible property.'

The following do not constitute 'property':

(1) information (*Oxford v Moss* (1979));

(2) electricity (*Low v Blease* (1975));

(3) a human corpse (*R v Sharpe* (1857)), except:

(a) if skill and effort have been exercised on it (*Doodeward v Spence* (1907));

(4) land; except appropriation by:

(a) a trustee, personal representative or liquidator;

(b) someone not in possession of anything severed from the land,

(c) a tenant of any fixture (s 4(2)(a)(b) and (c));

(5) wild plants, except:

(a) if the whole plant is taken;

(b) if taken for sale or reward (s 4(3));

(6) wild animals, except:

(a) if tamed or ordinarily kept in captivity;

(b) if reduced into someone's possession;

(c) if in the process of being reduced into someone's possession (s 4(4)).

Belonging to another

Section 5(1) defined 'belonging to another':

'Property shall be regarded as belonging to any person having possession or control of it, or having in it any proprietary right or interest ...'.

Section 5(3) extends the above definition:

'Where a person receives property from or on account of another, and is under an obligation to the other to retain and deal with that property or its proceeds in a particular way, the property or proceeds shall be regarded (as against him) as belonging to the other.'

Since the 'obligation' must be *legally enforceable* (*R v Gilks* (1972)), this will normally involve *contractual* obligations.

Section 5(4) covers the situation where the defendant receives property by mistake:

'Where a person gets property by another's mistake, and is under an obligation to make restitution ... then ... the property or proceeds shall be regarded (as against him) as belonging to the person entitled to restoration ...'.

If the mistake is fundamental the subsection is not of relevance as no property can pass under a void contract. Where the mistake is non-fundamental the contract will be voidable, but even in this case, it can be argued that the subsection is not relevant as there is no obligation to make restoration until the contract is actually avoided.

However, it does appear that the subsection will cover a *mistaken overpayment* by a bank or an employer (*Attorney General's Reference No 1 of 1983* (1984)).

Appropriation

Appropriation is defined in s 3(1) of the Theft Act 1968:

'Any assumption by a person of the rights of an owner amounts to an appropriation ...'.

The appropriation can, therefore, take many forms, including:

(1) offering the property for sale;

(2) taking the property;

(3) pledging the property;

(4) destroying the property;

(5) fixing the price of the property.

In *R v Gomez* (1992) the House of Lords decided that there can be an appropriation even though there is consent provided the consent is obtained by fraud or deception.

Mens rea

Dishonesty

Section 2(1) of the Theft Act 1968 provides that a person is *not* dishonest if he appropriates in the honest belief that:

(1) he has a legal right to deprive another of the property (s 2(1)(a));

(2) he would have the other's consent if the other knew of the appropriation and the circumstances of it (s 2(1)(b));

(3) the person to whom the property belongs cannot be discovered by taking reasonable steps (s 2(1)(c)).

In the case of *R v Ghosh* (1982), the Court of Appeal held that in cases of doubt as to dishonesty the jury should be given the following direction:

'Was the defendant dishonest according to the standards of ordinary decent people? If yes, did the defendant realise that what he was doing was dishonest by these standards?'

Intention to permanently deprive

By s 6(1) of the Theft Act 1968 a person will be deemed to have an intention to permanently deprive if it is his intention

'... to treat the thing as his own to dispose of regardless of the other's rights: and a borrowing or lending of it may amount to so treating it if, but only if, the borrowing or lending is for a period and in circumstances making it equivalent to an outright taking or disposal.'

Such a borrowing must result in the property *losing virtually all of its value* before a defendant will be deemed to have an intention to permanently deprive.

Under s 6(2) of the Theft Act 1968 where a person parts with property '... under a condition as to its return which he may not be able to perform ...' he will be deemed to have an intention to permanently deprive.

Robbery

Definition

Section 8(1) of the Theft Act 1968 provides:

> 'A person is guilty of robbery if he steals, and immediately before or at the time of doing so, and in order to do so, he uses force on any person or puts or seeks to put any person in fear of being then and there subjected to force.'

Force

Whether force has been used or threatened is a matter for the jury to decide (*R v Dawson* (1976)).

The force can be used or threatened against *any person*, not necessarily the owner of the property (*Smith v Desmond Hall* (1965)).

The force, or threat of force, must be used *in order to steal* (*R v Shendley* (1970)).

Stealing

All the elements required for s 1(1) theft are necessary to establish that the defendant has stolen for the purposes of robbery.

Burglary

Definition

Under s 9 of the Theft Act 1968 there are two forms of burglary, but both require that the defendant has entered a *building* or *part of a building* as a *trespasser*.

Building or part of a building

The following are relevant decisions on the question of what constitutes a building or part of a building:

(1) in *Stevens v Gourley* (1859) it was stated that a building was '... a structure of considerable size and intended to be permanent or at least to endure for a considerable length of time.';

(2) in *B and S v Leathley* (1979) a large freezer container standing in a farmyard without foundations was held to constitute a building;

(3) in *Norfolk Constabulary v Seekings and Gould* (1986) a lorry trailer, used for storage and connected to the electricity supply, was not held to be a building;

(4) in *R v Walkington* (1979) a customer who went behind a till counter was held to have entered part of a building as a trespasser.

Entry

The defendant must enter, or have entered, a building. An 'entry' must be *'substantial and effective'* (*R v Collins* (1973)).

In *R v Brown* (1985) it was held that leaning through a broken shop window in order to remove goods was sufficient to constitute an entry for the purposes of burglary.

'As a trespasser'

The defendant must not only enter a building, he must do so as a trespasser. A trespasser is someone who enters property without express or implied permission.

It will amount to trespass where the defendant *exceeds* the express or implied conditions of entry, for example, by entering a friend's house with an intention to steal (*R v Smith and Jones* (1976)).

The defendant must know or be reckless in the *Cunningham* sense as to whether his entry is trespassory (*R v Collins* (1973)).

Section 9(1)(a)

By s 9(1)(a) of the Theft Act 1968 a person is guilty of burglary if:

'... he enters any building or part of a building as a trespasser ...' with an intention to:

(1) steal;

(2) inflict grievous bodily harm;

(3) rape;

(4) commit unlawful damage to the building or anything therein.

Section 9(1)(b)

A person is guilty of this offence if having entered a building or part of a building as a trespasser he commits or attempts to:

(1) steal; or

(2) inflict grievous bodily harm.

Blackmail

Definition

Section 21(1) of the Theft Act 1968 provides:

'A person is guilty of blackmail if, with a view to gain for himself or another or with intent to cause loss to another, he makes any unwarranted demand with menaces ...'.

Scope

Section 24(4) of the Theft Act 1968 provides that property obtained as a result of blackmail is to be regarded as 'stolen goods' for the purposes of handling.

Where property is demanded with an accompanying threat of immediate violence there will be liability in relation to both robbery, contrary to s 8 and blackmail, contrary to s 21.

Actus reus

Demand

A demand can take the form of words or actions and can be express or implied, where it is obvious to the victim and would have been obvious to a reasonable person that a demand is being made (*R v Collister and Warhurst* (1955)).

Section 21(2) provides that the nature of the act or omission demanded is immaterial.

There is no need for the demand to reach the victim.

Menaces

The word menace is an ordinary English word which is normally left to the jury without any attempt at definition from the judge (*R v Lawrence* (1972)). It is clearly not limited to threats of violence, but is capable of including any action which is detrimental or unpleasant to the victim (*Thorne v Motor Trade Association* (1937)).

The Court of Appeal in *R v Clear* (1968) suggested that the approach for determining whether or not menaces have been made out should be to consider what effect the words or actions of the defendant would have had on a reasonable person. However, this test may be modified where there is evidence that the victim is unusually brave or timorous. In the former case, menaces are made out if a reasonable person would have been affected, in the latter case, where a reasonable person would have remained unaffected, menaces are still made out provided the defendant realised the effect of his actions on the victim (*R v Garwood* (1987)).

Mens rea

The demand must be made by the defendant either '... with a view to gain for himself or another, or with intent to cause loss to another' (s 21(1)). This provision has the effect of limiting the scope of blackmail to situations where the defendant acts to secure a 'gain' or 'loss' in money or other property (s 34(2)(a)).

A demand will not be 'unwarranted' if the defendant makes it in the honest belief (although not necessarily a reasonable belief) that he has reasonable grounds for doing so, and in the belief that the use of menaces is a proper means of reinforcing the demand.

Handling stolen goods

Definition

Section 22(1) of the Theft Act 1968 provides:

'A person handles stolen goods if (otherwise than in the course of the stealing) knowing or believing them to be stolen goods he dishonestly receives the goods, or dishonestly undertakes or assists in their retention, removal, disposal or realisation by or for the benefit of another.'

Actus reus

Goods

Section 34(2)(b) of the Theft Act 1968 states that 'goods' include:

'... money and every other description of property except land, and includes things severed from the land by stealing.'

Since '... every other description of property ...' includes choses in action as well as tangible property, a bank account into which money obtained in exchange for stolen property has been paid will constitute stolen goods (*R v Pritchley* (1973), *Attorney General's Reference No 4 of 1979* (1980)).

Stolen

In order to constitute stolen property the goods must have been obtained as a result of *theft, obtaining property by deception,* or *blackmail* (s 24(4) Theft Act 1968).

By s 24(3) goods will lose their 'stolen' status if:

'... restored to the person from whom they were stolen or to other lawful possession or custody ...'.

Thus, in *Haughton v Smith* (1975) tins of meat ceased to be 'stolen' when police took control of the lorry transporting them.

However, what amounts to 'custody' seems to depend on the degree of control exercised over the goods. In *Attorney General's Reference No 1 of 1974* (1974) the Court of Appeal were unwilling to hold that a police officer who immobilised a car that he suspected of containing stolen goods by removing its rotor arm had taken custody of the property.

If goods have ceased to be 'stolen' because they have been taken into lawful custody the defendant who handles them, believing them to be stolen, will be liable for *attempting* to handle stolen goods contrary to s 1(1) of the Criminal Attempts Act 1981 (*R v Shivpuri* (1985)).

Goods which represent stolen goods

Where the stolen goods have been exchanged for other forms of property, that other property may also constitute 'stolen goods'.

Section 24(2) provides that for goods to be stolen they must be, or have been, in the hands of the thief or handler and directly or indirectly represent the stolen goods in whole or in part.

Forms of handling

Receiving: taking possession of the stolen property. It is not necessary to show that the defendant acted 'for the benefit of another'.

Removal: moving the stolen goods from one place to another. The transportation must be 'for the benefit of another'.

Realisation: selling or exchanging the stolen goods. The realisation must be 'for the benefit of another'.

Disposal: destroying or hiding the stolen goods. The disposal must be 'for the benefit of another'.

Retention: keeping possession of the stolen goods. The retention must be 'for the benefit of another'. It seems that a mere omission to inform the police of the presence of stolen property will not amount to retention (*R v Brown* (1970)), whereas in *R v Kanwar* (1982) a defendant who deliberately misled the police as to the presence of stolen goods in her home was held to have assisted her husband in their retention.

In addition, it is also an offence under s 22(1) to arrange to do any of the above or arrange to assist in the removal, realisation, disposal or retention of stolen goods by another person.

For the benefit of another

All of the above forms of handling, with the exception of receiving and arranging to receive, require that the defendant act 'for the benefit another'. Thus, a defendant who knowingly sells stolen goods for his own benefit will not be liable for arranging, assisting or undertaking the realisation of stolen property. It seems that the innocent purchaser would not be 'another person' within the meaning of the subsection (*R v Bloxham* (1983)).

Otherwise than in the course of stealing

This phrase in the definition of the offence is intended to avoid an overlap between thieves and handlers. Without some such limitation virtually every case of handling could also be charged as theft. However, the extent to which the phrase succeeds in distinguishing the two offences is somewhat problematic.

One difficulty relates to whether appropriation in theft is considered to be an *instantaneous* or a *continuous* act. The case of *R v Pitham and Hehl* (1976) provides authority for the first proposition, whereas the Court of Appeal's decision in *R v Hale* (1978) supports the second. It is only where the continuous act concept of appropriation is accepted that the 'otherwise than in the course of stealing' provision makes sense. However, if this continuing act concept of appropriation is accepted there then occurs the problem of determining when it should end. The practical approach seems to be to leave it to the jury to decide on the basis of the facts in the case. The important point to remember is that liability for handling contrary to s 22 cannot commence until the continuing act has terminated.

Another difficulty that is sometimes alleged relates to whom the phrase applies. It can be argued that *all* those who knowingly deal with the stolen goods satisfy both the *actus reus* and *mens rea* requirements for s 1 theft and are consequently within the course of 'stealing'. If this argument were accepted it would be very difficult to secure convictions for handling, consequently the Court of Appeal in *R v Sainthouse* (1980) suggested that the 'course of stealing' be restricted to the initial theft by which the goods become 'stolen'.

Figure 17 Forms of handling

FORM	ACTION	BENEFIT OF ANOTHER	OMISSION
Receiving	Taking into possession or control	Not necessary	
Removal	Movement of goods		Action required
Realisation	Sale or exchange	Must be for another's benefit	
Disposal	Destroying or hiding		
Retention	Keeping		Possible by omission

Mens rea

Dishonesty

The issue of dishonesty will be left to the jury to decide. The Court of Appeal decision in *R v Roberts* (1987) indicates that the test for establishing dishonesty laid down in *R v Ghosh* (1982) should not be automatically applied, but reserved for cases of difficulty.

Knowledge or belief that the goods are stolen

In addition to dishonesty, the prosecution must prove that the defendant knew or believed the goods to be stolen.

Belief is a purely subjective matter and should not be equated with what the reasonable person would have believed in the same circumstances (*Atwal v Massey* (1971)).

A jury is entitled to *infer* belief where there was evidence that should have made the defendant suspect that the goods were stolen (*R v Lincoln* (1980)), although mere suspicion is not to be *equated* with belief (*R v Grainge* (1974)).

Similarly, in the absence of a satisfactory explanation, a jury is entitled to *infer* belief where there is evidence that the defendant came into possession of the goods soon after the theft.

Obtaining property by deception

Definition

Section 15(1) of the Theft Act 1968 provides:

'A person who by any deception dishonestly obtains property belonging to another, with the intention of permanently depriving the other of it, shall on conviction on indictment be liable to imprisonment ...'

Actus reus

Property belonging to another

Section 34(1) of the Theft Act 1968 provides that s 4(1) and s 5(1) relating to property belonging to another should apply generally for the purposes of the Act. The concepts of 'property' and 'belonging to another', therefore, have a similar meaning to that already noted in relation to s 1.

Obtaining

Section 15(2) provides:

'For the purposes of this section a person is to be treated as obtaining property if he obtains ownership, possession or control of it and "obtains" includes obtaining for another or enabling another to obtain or to retain.'

Clearly the *actus reus* of the offence will be committed where the defendant induces the victim to *sell*, *give* or *loan* property. However, it seems that the offence would *not* be committed where the defendant by deception is allowed to *retain* property of which he already had possession or control. The appropriate charge in these circumstances would be one of theft, by virtue of s 3(1).

Deception

Section 15(4) provides:

'For purposes of this section "deception" means any deception (whether deliberate or reckless) by words or conduct as to fact or as to law, including a deception as to the present intentions of the person using the deception or any other person.'

The following points should be noted:

(1) a statement of opinion cannot amount to a deception;

(2) to constitute a deception the statement must be untrue;

(3) conduct can amount to a deception (*DPP v Ray* (1974));

(4) a machine cannot be deceived (*Davies v Flackett* (1972)).

Causation

The deception must be *operative*; ie it must cause the obtaining of the property. It follows that the 'but for' test and the other rules relating to causation, noted above, are relevant to s 15.

In *DPP v Ray* (above) the defendant waited at a table in a restaurant until the waiters had left the room before running out without paying. It was held that his conduct of remaining at the table was a continuing representation that he was an honest customer who intended to pay the bill. This deception was operative because it induced the waiters to leave the dining area unattended, giving him the opportunity to leave without paying.

In *R v Collis-Smith* (1971) a defendant, having filled his car with petrol, falsely told a garage attendant that his employer would pay. On appeal it was held that the deception could not have been operative because it was not made until *after* the property in the petrol had already passed to the defendant. The appropriate charge in these circumstances would have been under s 2 of the 1978 Theft Act (see below).

Mens rea

The *mens rea* required for obtaining property by deception contrary to s 15(1) consists of three elements:

(1) the defendant must *intend* to deceive or be *reckless* (in the *Cunningham* sense) as to whether he deceives;

(2) the defendant must be *dishonest* and in cases of doubt, the model direction laid down in *R v Ghosh* (1982) should be given to the jury (however, the negative definition of dishonesty contained in s 2(1) does not apply to deception offences);

(3) the defendant must have an *intention to permanently deprive* (a defendant may be deemed to have such an intention in situations specified by s 6(1) and (2)).

Obtaining a pecuniary advantage by deception

Definition

Section 16(1) of the Theft Act 1968, as amended, provides:

'A person who by any deception dishonestly obtains for himself or another any pecuniary advantage shall on conviction on indictment be liable to imprisonment for a term not exceeding five years.'

Actus reus

Once more the deception must cause the obtaining of the pecuniary advantage. Moreover, 'deception', 'obtaining' and causation all have the same meaning as for s 15.

'Pecuniary advantage' does *not* include any financial benefit, but is limited to the following very specific situations:

(1) being allowed to borrow by way of overdraft (see, for example, *CMP v Charles* (1977) and *R v Lambie* (1982));

(2) taking out a policy of insurance or annuity contract, or obtaining an improvement of the terms on which the defendant is allowed to do so;

(3) being given an opportunity to earn remuneration or greater remuneration;

(4) being given the opportunity to win money by betting.

Mens rea

The requisite *mens rea* consists of two elements:

(1) the defendant must *intend* to deceive or be *reckless* (in the *Cunningham* sense) as to whether he deceives another;

(2) the defendant must be *dishonest* at the time of the obtaining (as with s 15, the *Ghosh* direction should be given in cases of doubt).

False accounting

Definition

Section 17(1) of the Theft Act 1968 provides:

> 'Where a person dishonestly, with a view to gain for himself or another or with intent to cause loss to another:
>
> (a) destroys, defaces, conceals or falsifies any account or any record or document made or required for any accounting purpose; or
>
> (b) in furnishing information for any purpose produces or makes use of any account, or any such record or document as aforesaid, which to his knowledge is or may be misleading, false or deceptive in a material particular;
>
> he shall, on conviction on indictment, be liable to imprisonment for a term not exceeding seven years.'

Actus reus

'Accounting' is interpreted as *financial* accounting although accounting in this sense need not be the only purpose for which the document is produced.

Section 17(2) provides that a person who makes:

> '... an entry which is or may be misleading, false or deceptive in a material

particular, or who omits or concurs in omitting a material particular from an account or other document, is to be treated as falsifying the account or document.'

Mens rea

The *mens rea* consists of dishonesty together with a '... view to gain for himself or another, or with intent to cause loss to another ...'.

Additionally, in relation to s 17(1)(b), the defendant must *know* that the document is or may be misleading, false or deceptive in a material particular, or he must be *reckless* (in the *Cunningham* sense) in this regard.

Obtaining services by deception

Definition

Section 1(1) of the Theft Act 1978 provides:

'A person who by any deception dishonestly obtains services from another shall be guilty of an offence.'

Actus reus

Section 1(2) defines a 'service' in terms of a 'benefit':

'It is an obtaining of services where the other is induced to confer a benefit by doing some act, or causing or permitting some act to be done, on the understanding that the benefit has been or will be paid for.'

It seems that virtually anything is capable of being a 'benefit' if it is something that an individual would be willing to pay for.

Clearly, gratuitous services are excluded from the scope of the offence by the words '... on the understanding that the benefit has been or will be paid for ...'.

The deception must precede the obtaining of the service, and must be operative in that it causes the provision of the service.

Section 5(1) of the Theft Act 1978 provides that 'deception' has the same meaning as in s 15 of the 1968 Theft Act (see above).

Mens rea

The defendant must *intend* to deceive or be *reckless* (in the *Cunningham* sense) as to the deception. In addition, the defendant must be dishonest at the time of the obtaining of the service.

Where dishonesty is in doubt the '*Ghosh*' direction should be given to the jury.

Evasion of liability by deception

Section 2 of the Theft Act 1978 creates three offences of evasion of liability by deception. It would appear that these three offences are not mutually exclusive (*R v Holt* (1981)).

Securing remission of liability by deception

Definition

Section 2(1)(a) of the Theft Act 1978 provides:

'... where a person by any deception dishonestly secures the remission of the whole or part of any existing liability to make a payment, whether his own liability or another's, he shall be guilty of an offence.'

Actus reus

As is common to all the deception offences, the deception must be operative in that it must cause the securing of the remission of liability.

The 'liability' in question must be an existing legal liability to pay. It will, therefore, almost inevitably, refer to a contractual obligation or judgment debt.

It would appear that the words 'secured the remission' of the liability denote nothing less than the total extinguishing of the legal liability to pay. However, it can be argued, as a matter of civil law, that an existing liability can never be extinguished by a deception. This is because any agreement to extinguish liability will be rendered void, or at least, voidable, by deception and, therefore, will not be totally extinguished. If this argument is correct, it is difficult to see how anyone could ever be liable in relation to s 1(2).

Mens rea

The defendant must *intend* to deceive, or be *reckless* (in the *Cunningham* sense) as to the deception. In addition, the defendant must be dishonest at the time of securing the remission of the liability to pay.

Delaying payment by deception

Definition

Section 2(1)(b) of the Theft Act 1978 provides:

'Where a person by any deception with intent to make permanent default in whole or in part on any existing liability to make a payment, or with intent to let another do so, dishonestly induces the creditor or any person claiming payment on behalf of the creditor to wait for payment (whether or not the due date for payment is deferred) or to forgo payment, he shall be guilty of an offence.'

Actus reus

Clearly, the offence is aimed at the defendant who delays paying his creditor by deception whilst having a secret intention never to pay the debt.

The comments concerning 'deception' and 'liability' made in relation to s 2(1)(a), above, also apply to s 2(1)(b).

Section 2(3) provides that:

'... a person induced to take in payment a cheque or other security for money by way of conditional satisfaction of a pre-existing liability is to be treated not as being paid but as being induced to wait for payment.'

The offence would, therefore, be committed where the defendant pays for goods or services with a cheque which he knows will be dishonoured.

Mens rea

The defendant must *intend* to deceive, or be *reckless* (in the *Cunningham* sense) as to the deception. As with s 2(1)(a), the defendant must also be dishonest, however, there must be an additional intention to never pay the debt.

Obtaining exemption from or abatement of liability by deception

Definition

Section 2(1)(c) of the Theft Act 1978 provides:

'Where any person by any deception dishonestly obtains any exemption from or abatement of liability to make a payment he shall be guilty of an offence.'

Actus reus

The main difference between this offence and the other two offences under s 2 is that 'liability' includes not merely existing obligations, but also future liabilities (*R v Frith* (1990)).

Mens rea

The defendant must *intend* to deceive, or be *reckless* (in the *Cunningham* sense) as to the deception. In addition, the defendant must be *dishonest*, but, unlike s 2(1)(b), no *intention* to make permanent default need be established.

Making off without payment

Definition

Section 3(1) of the Theft Act 1978 provides:

'... a person who, knowing that payment on the spot for any goods supplied or service done is required or expected from him, dishonestly makes off without having paid as required or expected and with intent to avoid payment of the amount due shall be guilty of an offence.'

Actus reus

Section 3(3) provides that the offence will not be committed if:

'... the supply of the goods or the doing of the service is contrary to law, or where the service done is such that payment is not legally enforceable.'

The defendant must have 'made off' by leaving the premises where payment is due (*R v McDavitt* (1981)).

Failing to pay includes leaving an inadequate amount, counterfeit notes or foreign currency. It would also include using another's cheque or credit card or leaving a cheque that will be dishonoured.

Mens rea

The *mens rea* for this offence consists of three elements:

(1) *knowledge* that payment on the spot is required;

(2) *dishonesty*;

(3) *intention* to permanently avoid payment (*R v Allen* (1985)).

General defences

Infancy

Infants are persons under the age of 18. For the purposes of the criminal law they can be divided into three categories:

(1) children under 10 who are entirely exempt from criminal responsibility;

(2) children over 9 and under 14 were traditionally exempt from criminal responsibility unless the prosecution could prove not only the *actus reus* and *mens rea* for the crime in question, but also that the child acted with 'mischievous discretion' (ie that the child knew what he was doing was seriously wrong (*R v Gorrie* (1919)). However, the Divisional Court has recently held that this rebuttable presumption in no longer part of English law (*C (a Minor) v DPP* (1994);

(3) those over 14 who can be criminally liable on proof of *actus reus* and *mens rea* in the same way that adults can.

Insanity

Relevance

Insanity may become relevant in three situations:

(1) where the defendant has been committed in custody for trial;

(2) when the defendant is brought up for trial and is found unfit to plead; and

(3) when insanity is raised as a defence during the trial.

Definition

The definition of insanity is based upon the *M'Naghten rules* laid down in 1843. It must be proved (by the defence, on a balance of probabilities) that at the time the offence was committed the defendant was labouring under such a defect of reason, arising from a disease of the mind, so as not to know the nature and quality of the act he was doing, or, if he did know it, that he did not know that what he was doing was wrong.

Disease of the mind

According to Lord Denning in *Bratty v Attorney General for Northern Ireland* (1963) a 'disease of the mind' can be a disease of the body that affects the mind in a manner which manifests itself in violence and is likely to recur.

One way the courts have distinguished between insanity and automatism is by accepting that a disease of the mind is likely to be caused by *internal* factors (eg the disease of diabetes in *R v Hennessy* (1989)) while automatism will generally result from *external* factors acting upon the body (eg insulin taken to stabilise the metabolism of a diabetic in *R v Quick* (1973)). The decision of the House of Lords in *R v Sullivan* (1984) provides support for this approach.

Acts done while sleep-walking have been held to have an internal cause and consequently amount to insane rather than non-insane automatism (*R v Burgess* (1991)).

The nature and quality of the act

One of the two grounds for establishing insanity under the *M'Naghten rules* is that the defendant's disease of the mind prevented him from being aware of his actions. For example, in *R v Kemp* (1957) the defendant was found not guilty by reason of insanity when he was unaware of his actions during a 'blackout' caused by a disease of the body which affected the mind.

Did not know that the action was wrong

The second ground for establishing the defence is that, because of a disease of the mind, the defendant did not know that his actions were wrong.'Wrong' in this context has been interpreted to mean *legally* as opposed to morally wrong (*R v Windle* (1952)).

Mistake of fact

Mistake of fact is a defence where it prevents the defendant from forming the *mens rea* for the crime in question. The mistake must be honest, but it need not be reasonable (*DPP v Morgan* (1976)).

Where the law requires negligence, then only a reasonable mistake can afford a defence.

Where strict liability is imposed even a reasonable mistake will not excuse.

Intoxication

Voluntary intoxication

Self-induced intoxication must be considered in relation to two categories:

(1) intoxication by alcohol and dangerous drugs where evidence of self-induced intoxication negativing *mens rea* is a defence to crimes of *specific* intent, but not to crimes of *basic* intent (*DPP v Majewski* (1977));

(2) intoxication otherwise than by alcohol or dangerous drugs where liability for crimes of *basic* intent will depend upon whether the defendant has been reckless or not (*R v Bailey* (1983); *R v Hardie* (1984)).

Where the defendant deliberately becomes intoxicated in order to gain 'dutch courage' the defence will not be available even in relation to crimes of *specific* intent (*Attorney General for Northern Ireland v Gallagher* (1963)).

Involuntary intoxication

Involuntary intoxication which negates *mens rea* will be a defence to crimes of both basic and specific intent. Indeed, following *R v Kingston* (1993) it now seems that the defence will be available even if the defendant formed an intention to commit the offence, provided there is evidence that he would not have done so, but for the drink.

According to the decision of the Court of Appeal in *R v Allen* (1988), if the defendant knows that he is drinking alcohol, but is mistaken as to its strength, the rules relating to *voluntary* intoxication will be applied.

Necessity

The nature of the defence

The defence of necessity is based on a plea that the defendant committed the crime in question, but did so in order to avoid a greater evil.

Availability

For policy reasons the English courts have been reluctant to accept the defence of necessity. In *R v Dudley and Stephens* (1884) is was decided that necessity could not found a valid defence to a homicide charge. This principle has received the support of the House of Lords in *R v Howe* (1987).

Statutory examples of necessity

However, the defence has appeared in various statutory provisions although not always explicitly:

(1) s 5(2)(b) of the Criminal Damage Act 1971 provides that it is a lawful excuse for damaging property if it is done in order to protect other property and

that the defendant believes that such action must be taken immediately, and that it is reasonable in the circumstances;

(2) s 1(1) of the Infant Life (Preservation) Act 1929 provides a defence if the death of the child was caused in good faith for the purpose of preserving the life of the mother;

(3) s 1(4) of the Abortion Act 1967 provides that a qualified medical practitioner can lawfully terminate a pregnancy where:

'... he is of the opinion, formed in good faith, that the termination is immediately necessary to save the life or to prevent grave permanent injury to the physical or mental health of the pregnant woman.'

Necessity at common law

The courts have been prepared in a series of cases to accept the defence of necessity, albeit under the guise of 'duress of circumstances', at least in road traffic situations:

(1) *R v Willer* (1986);

(2) *R v Conway* (1989);

(3) *R v Martin* (1989).

On the basis of *Conway* and *Martin* it appears that where the defendant was constrained to drive to avoid death or serious injury the jury should be directed as follows:

(1) had the defendant felt compelled to act by what he perceived to be the grave danger of the situation? If so;

(2) would a sober person of reasonable firmness sharing the characteristics of the accused have responded to the perceived threat by acting as the accused had?

If the answers to both these questions are in the affirmative, the defence of necessity, always assuming it to be available, will be established.

Duress

Definition

The defence of duress consists of a plea that the defendant felt compelled to commit a crime because of an immediate threat of death or serious bodily harm.

Availability

Duress is not available to the following:

(1) some forms of treason;

(2) murder (*R v Howe* (1987));

(3) attempted murder (*R v Gotts* (1991)).

Criminal groups voluntarily joined

The defence of duress is not available to those who voluntarily join criminal groups and are then forced to commit the type of crime for which the group is renowned (*R v Sharp* (1987)).

However, if the defendant is forced to commit an offence of a type which he could not have been expected to foresee when he joined the criminal organisation he still may be able to rely on the defence (*R v Shepard* (1988)).

The direction for duress

The Court of Appeal in *R v Graham* (1982) laid down the direction that should be given to the jury where the defendant has raised the defence of duress. This direction has subsequently been approved by the House of Lords in *R v Howe* (1987) and can be summarised as follows:

(1) was the defendant compelled to act as he did because, on the basis of the circumstances as he honestly believed them to be, he thought his life was in immediate danger? If so;

(2) would a sober person of reasonable firmness sharing the defendant's characteristics have responded in the same way to the threats?

If the answers to both these questions is 'yes' the defence of duress is established. The above direction is very similar to those we have already noted for establishing both necessity and provocation.

Coercion

Coercion is a special defence available only to a wife who commits an offence (other than treason or murder) in the presence of, and under the coercion of, her husband.

Coercion, unlike duress, can consist of 'pressure' as well as threats of physical violence (*R v Richman* (1982)).

Public and private defence

Relevant situations

It is a defence to use *reasonable* force to defend certain public and private interests:

(1) defence of property under s 5 of the Criminal Damage Act 1971;

(2) arrest and prevention of crime under s 3 of the Criminal Law Act 1967;

(3) self-defence under the common law.

Reasonable force

Generally, the law allows such force as is *reasonable* in the circumstances.

However, s 5(3) of the Criminal Damage Act 1971 provides a more extensive defence in that '... it is immaterial whether a belief (including a belief as to what is reasonable) is justified or not if it is honestly held ...'. However, it seems that there are limits as to how far the courts are prepared to take this. For example, in *Blake v DPP* (1993), it was held that the defendant's honest belief that he was acting with the consent and authority of God was not a defence.

In *R v Williams (Gladstone)* (1984) it was established that the defendant commits no offence if the force used was reasonable in the circumstances *as he believed them to be*.

The *Gladstone Williams* principle may have been extended by the decision in *R v Scarlett* (1993) where it seems that the court took the *defendant*'s view of what was reasonable in the circumstances as he believed them to be, rather the jury's.

Consent

Scope of the defence

Consent is a complete defence to theft, criminal damage and rape.

The law allows the defence of consent in relation to *medical treatment* (carried out by a qualified medical practitioner) and *sports* (played according to the rules).

Where two or more people fight (other than in the course of an organised sport) the defence of consent will *not* be allowed (*Attorney General's Reference No 6 of 1980* (1981)).

In the case of *R v Brown and Others* (1993), the majority of the House of Lords were prepared to regard consent as a defence to common and indecent assault, but were not prepared to extend the defence to the *deliberate* infliction of bodily harm (except in recognised cases, most notably boxing).

Consent and mistake

An honest belief (but not necessarily a reasonable belief) that the victim was consenting will negate the *mens rea* of the defendant (*R v Kimber* (1983)). Of course, the offence in question must be one where the defence of consent is recognised.

Consent obtained by deception

If the consent of the victim was obtained by deception it will be a *valid* consent provided it relates to a *non-fundamental* matter, but will be *void* where it relates to a *fundamental* matter (*R v Williams* (1923)).

A fundamental mistake occurs where the victim consents to something which is *qualitatively* different to that which he thought he was consenting to.

Strict liability

Definition

An offence of strict liability is one that does not require proof of fault.

Statutory interpretation

Where a statute creates a criminal offence, but fails to specify any requisite *mens rea*, the courts *presume* that Parliament intended the offence to involve proof of fault, unless there is clear evidence to the contrary (*per* Lord Scarman in *Gammon (Hong Kong) Ltd v Attorney General of Hong Kong* (1984)).

Even when a court decides that *mens rea* is required, it may not be necessary for the prosecution to prove it in relation to every element of the *actus reus* (*R v Lemon and Gay News Ltd* (1979)).

In deciding whether or not to impose strict liability the courts will have regard to the statute as a whole. If a section creating a particular offence is silent as to *mens rea* whereas other offences under the same Act expressly requires proof of fault then the court is entitled to conclude that the offence is one of strict liability (*Kirkland v Robinson* (1987)).

Generally, the more serious the offence the less likely the courts are to impose strict liability.

Where the offence is regarded as 'regulatory' or 'quasi-criminal' the courts are more prepared to impose strict liability (*Pharmaceutical Society of Great Britain v Storkwain* (1986)).

The courts will be reluctant to impose strict liability where there is evidence that the offence was committed despite the defendant having taken all reasonable care (*Sherras v De Rutzen* (1895)).

The courts are more likely to impose strict liability if they view the potential harm to society posed by the defendant's conduct to be greater than any injustice to the individual resulting from liability without fault.

The Law Commission has recommended that Parliament should expressly state whether an offence is one of strict liability (*Report on the Mental Element in Crime* ((1978) *Law Com* No 89) and a clause to that effect has been included in the Draft Criminal Code Bill (*C 20 Draft Criminal Code 1985*).

Possession of controlled drugs

Following the rather confused decision of the House in Lords in *Warner v MPC* (1970) and the subsequent enactment of the Misuse of Drugs Act 1971 it seems that the courts will impose a degree of strict liability in relation to the possession of controlled drugs.

Section 5 of the Misuse of Drugs Act 1971 creates the offence of possessing a controlled drug. To constitute this offence all the prosecution have to prove is that the defendant knew that he was in possession of a container holding 'something', and that in fact it held a controlled drug (*R v McNamara* (1988)). However, s 28(3)(b)(i) of the Act provides that a defendant should be acquitted if:

'... he proves that he neither believed nor suspected nor had reason to suspect that the substance ... in question was a controlled drug.'

In *Sweet v Parsley* (1970) the defendant was convicted of '... being concerned in the management of premises used for the smoking of cannabis' contrary to s 5(1)(b) of the Dangerous Drugs Act 1965. The House of Lords quashed her conviction on the grounds that since the offence was serious or 'truly criminal' proof of *mens rea* was required. Moreover, it was impractical to expect landlords to know everything that their tenants were doing.

Index